Mapping Sk[ills]
Activities and Outlines

Grades 4-8

Written by Ruth Solski and Lisa Solski
Illustrated by Ric Ward

ISBN 1-55035-759-X
Copyright 2004
Revised January 2006
All Rights Reserved * Printed in Canada

Published in the United States by:
On the Mark Press
3909 Witmer Road PMB 175
Niagara Falls, New York
14305
www.onthemarkpress.com

Published in Canada by:
S&S Learning Materials
15 Dairy Avenue
Napanee, Ontario
K7R 1M4
www.sslearning.com

At a Glance™

Learning Expectations	Mapping Skills Booklet				Activity Cards			
	What is a Map?	Kinds of Maps	Map Symbols	Day & Night, Seasons	Basic Mapping Skills	Wold Mapping Skills	Mapping Word Study	Outline Maps
Understanding Concepts								
• Become familiar with the types of maps used to identify different aspects of a country			●					
• Identify the four hemispheres and locate them on a globe or map				●				
• Understand the causes and effects of day and night, and the seasons				●	●			
• Locate and identify objects, and give directions in their environment using the cardinal and intermediate directions						●		
• Have a good understanding of, and use meridians of longitude and parallels of latitude to describe location					●		●	
Map anb Globe Skills								
• Locate and identify features on a map using the cardinal and intermediate directions					●	●		
• Use maps and the globe to locate countries, places, and physical features	●					●		●
• Read maps by using the symbols listed in a legend or key					●	●		
• Create sketch maps of familiar places, using symbols for places and routes					●			
• Use number and letter grids to locate places					●	●		
• Measure distances using a scale					●			
Communication Skills								
• Use appropriate vocabulary and terms while reading and making maps	●	●	●	●	●	●	●	●

Mapping Skills

Table of Contents

Mapping Skills

Teacher Assessment Rubric

Student's Name: _____

Criteria	Level 1	Level 2	Level 3	Level 4	Level
Understanding Concepts					
• Understands the concepts introduced.	A few	Some	Most	All/almost all	
• Gives complete explanations independently without relying on teacher prompts.	Rarely	Sometimes	Usually	Always/almost always	
Map and Globe Skills					
• Successfully applies required skills.	A few	Some	Most	All/almost all	
• Applies skills independently without teacher assistance.	Rarely	Sometimes	Usually	Always/almost always	
Communication Skills					
• Uses correct mapping and globe vocabulary introduced.	Rarely	Sometimes	Usually	Always/almost always	
• Communicates clearly, accurately, and with details.	Rarely	Sometimes	Usually	Always/almost always	

Comments: _____

_____

_____

_____

_____

_____

_____

_____

Mapping Skills
Student Self-Assessment Rubric

Name: _____   Date: _____

Put a check mark in each box that most accurately describes your performance, then add your points to determine your total score.

Expectations	Actual Performance (measured in points)				
	1 - Needs Improvement	2 - Sometimes	3 - Frequently	4 - Always/almost always	Points
Understanding Concepts					
I successfully identified, described, and explained the concepts introduced by my teacher.					
I gave complete explanations of concepts, independently without assistance from my teacher.					
Map and Globe Skills					
I read, used, and made maps correctly using symbols, grids, and the cardinal and intermediate directions.					
I read, used, and made maps accurately on my own without requiring help from my teacher or classmates.					
Communication Skills					
I used the correct vocabulary when talking and writing about a subject.					
I was clear, accurate, and gave lots of detail when I talked and wrote about a subject, and when I made maps.					

Total Points: _____

Questions for personal reflection:

1. What did you find most interesting, and enjoy learning about the most?

2. What questions do you have now, and what would you like to learn more about?

3. What can you improve upon, and how can you make this improvement?

Mapping Skills Activities

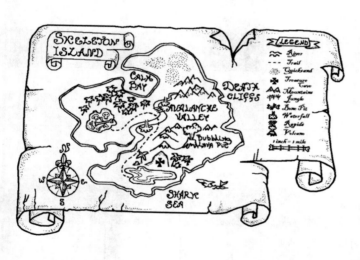

Mapping Skills

Preliminary Preparations

Collect the following items well in advance of the unit: a large wall map of the world; a large wall map of North America; several globes; compasses; atlases; books pertaining to maps and mapping, road maps of your province or state; different types of maps that show physical features, vegetation areas, mineral resources, types of industries, populated areas, location of animal life, climate, political divisions; local maps; transit maps; railroad maps; community maps; school maps; puzzle maps; old maps; nautical charts; reproducible maps for student usage; walking tours; films; filmstrips; videos; computer games. In addition, make Cardinal Direction Cards and post them in your classroom for all to see and use.

Introduction Ideas

1. Before beginning this book, make sure that your students are familiar with the cardinal and intermediate directions found on a compass and a compass rose. Ask your students if they could give oral directions to the location of their home, their school or another street in their neighborhood. If they are not familiar with the cardinal and intermediate directions, take them outside at noon on a sunny day. Make sure that you have chosen a well lit spot in the playground. Have the students spread out so that they have room to stretch their arms out to the side without touching one another. Once the students are in position, have them note in which direction their shadow is pointing. The students are to stand in that direction. Tell your students that their shadow always points to the north at noon in North America.

    Give the following directions:

    a) Raise your right arm and point to the right. This direction is east.
    b) Raise you left arm and point in the opposite direction. Your left arm is now pointing west.
    c) Look behind you to find south.

2. Play games with your students such as "Simon Says" or have them move about in different directions. Play "I Spy" and have the students use the directions so others can locate the object that is seen by the student.

3. Display different types of maps and books that pertain to maps on a display table, and allow the students to peruse the articles a week in advance of the book.

4. Locate a good poem that pertains to a map, globe or traveling around the world. Record the poem on a chart and have the students read it.

5. Locate a good adventure story to a far off land to read to your students. Have them locate the country on the map of the world.

6. Blindfold a student. Have a second student lead him or her from point A to point B. Keep the path simple, with only one or two turns at the most.

e.g. A chair chair table B = 13 steps

Return the blindfolded student to point A. The student must then duplicate the path as closely as possible.

Skills: counting step, noting turns, following directions that are not visual.

Mapping Skills

Bulletin Board Ideas

1. On a bulletin board display an historical map and a modern map. Discuss the maps with your students and compare them.

2. Display different types of maps for one country (preferably your own) in an interesting manner on the bulletin board. If you have access to an atlas that is falling apart, tear out the maps, mount them on a sturdy backing and laminate them. Print the name of the type of map on a label card and pin it near the map. For example: Physical Features, Vegetation, Location of Population, Mineral Resources, Political Map, etc.

3. Display a large map of your city, town or local community. The students may locate symbols that represent features on the map legend. They may also locate streets, buildings, parks, etc. This map may also be used to strengthen cardinal and intermediate directions.

4. Locate a large wall map of the world. Use pictures of famous world landmarks and have the students locate where they are found on the map. For example: Statue of Liberty - New York City, New York State, U.S.A.; CN Tower - Toronto, Ontario, Canada; Eiffel Tower - Paris, France; Buckingham Palace - London, England.

Teacher Input Suggestions

1. Use the reproducible booklet to teach the various aspects that pertain to maps and globes. Discuss the following topics and complete the work sheet page in the booklet as a follow-up to the lesson.

2. The information included in the unit will help to provide you with material on the topic. This information may be reproduced and given to the students to read along with the teacher, or it may be put on overheads and read with the entire class.

3. Discuss the following topics:
   a) What is a map?
   b) Why are maps important?
   c) What do maps tell us?
   d) Who makes maps?
   e) Kinds of maps
   f) Directional indicators
   g) Map symbols
   h) A legend or key
   i) Scale and measuring distance
   j) What is a globe? Why is it important? How are globes used?
   k) Hemispheres
   l) Lines on a globe - Parallels of latitude and meridians of longitude
   m) Day and night
   n) The seasons

4. The reproducible work sheets may be used as activity cards or reproduced for student usage. The activities are to be completed after all the content has been taught to reinforce many of the skills required to develop accurate map reading.

Mapping Skills

5. The Basic Map Reading Skills Cards (p. 31) should be used before the World Map Reading Skills Cards (p.46) if your students do not have any background knowledge or experience working with mapping skills. The Basic Map Reading Skills Cards may also be used as a review of the previously learned skills.

6. Some of the cards may be worked on independently while others would be better used in a large group setting to help students who are experiencing difficulty.

Glossary of Geographic Terms

altitude: the height or elevation above sea level.

Antarctic Circle: an imaginary line of latitude 66° 30' (66 degrees 30 minutes) south of the equator.

aphelion: the time of year when the earth is farthest from the sun.

archipelago: a group or chain of islands.

Arctic Circle: an imaginary line of latitude 66° 30' north of the equator.

atlas: a book of maps that represents the many areas of the earth's surface. It may also include maps of the other planets within the solar system.

axis: the diameter upon which the earth rotates.

bay: a part of an ocean, sea, or lake extending into land.

bank: the sloping ground bordering a stream, lake or other body of water; a shallow part of the ocean.

basin: a depression or hollow which may or may not contain water, surrounded by higher land.

brook: a small, natural stream of fresh water.

canal: a narrow, man-made waterway used for ships or irrigation.

canyon: a deep, narrow valley with steep, sloping sides.

cape (or point): a point of land extending into a body of water.

cardinal directions: the four compass directions – north, south, east and west – which are read along the meridians and parallels on the globe.

channel: a narrow passage of water between two land masses that connects two large bodies of water; also the deepest part of a river or harbor.

cliff: a steep, high wall of rock along a coast, river or lake.

coast: the land bordering the sea, the seashore.

compass directions: the directions away from any given place based upon magnetic north.

compass rose: the design which shows the directions on a map; the north and south "petals" are usually longer than the east, west and intermediate "petals".

Mapping Skills

continent: any one of the earth's seven large land masses such as North America, South America, Europe, Asia, Africa, Australia, Antarctica.

contour map: a map that uses contour lines to show land that is uneven; the space between the lines indicates the steepness of the slope of the land.

day: the approximate time for one rotation of the earth - 24 hours.

degree: one of the 360 units of measurement which make up a circle, represented by the symbol °. Degrees are subdivided into 60 minutes, represented by the symbol'.

delta: a triangular or fan-shaped area of soil that has been carried downstream and dropped at a river's mouth.

depression: a land area that is lower than the surrounding ground. A depression is often below sea level.

desert: a land area so dry that little or no plant life will grow. Very few people live in a desert.

diameter: a line passing through the center of a sphere.

distortion: the stretching or compressing of parts of a map when it is transferred from the globe to a flat plane.

down: toward the center of the earth.

east: the direction along a parallel toward the rising sun.

eastern hemisphere: the half of the earth that includes Africa, Asia, Australia, Europe and their waters.

elevation: the height or distance above sea level.

equator: an imaginary line of latitude (0°), halfway between the North and South Poles.

equinoxes: the two times of the year, usually about March 21 and September 21, when the sun's rays are perpendicular to the equator, and day and night are of equal length everywhere.

glacier: a large body of ice that moves slowly down a mountainside or along a valley toward sea level.

globe: the only true world map, made on a ball or sphere the shape of the earth.

Greenwich meridian: the meridian passing through the borough of Greenwich in London, England, now used as 0° longitude (the prime meridian) from which time around the world is calculated.

grid: the network of meridians and parallels on a map.

gulf: a large arm of an ocean or sea partly surrounded by land.

hemisphere: any half of the earth's surface.

highland: a high or hilly point of land.

hill: a slightly higher point of land rising above the surrounding land.

horizon: the line where the earth's surface and the sky seem to meet.

ice shelf: a thick, floating area of ice lying next to a land area.

intermediate directions: the directions on the compass which fall between two of the cardinal directions; northeast, southeast, southwest, northwest.

island: an area of land, smaller than a continent, completely surrounded by water.

isthmus: a narrow strip of land located between two water bodies, connecting two large land areas.

International Date Line: an imaginary line of longitude generally 180° east or west of the prime meridian. The date becomes one day earlier to the east of the line.

lagoon: a shallow area of water separated from the ocean by a sandbank or by a strip of low land.

lake: a body of fresh or salt water entirely surrounded by land.

land hemisphere: the hemisphere with the maximum land area, roughly centered on northern France.

latitude: the distance, measured in degrees, north or south of the equator.

longitude: the distance, measured in degrees, east or west of the prime meridian.

map: a drawing of all or a part of the earth.

meridian: an imaginary line of longitude running between the North Pole and the South Pole.

minute: one of 60 equal parts of a degree.

mountain: an unusually high elevation rising steeply above its surroundings.

north: the directions along a meridian toward the North Pole and North Star.

North Pole: the point farthest north on the earth's surface. It is 90° north of the equator.

northern hemisphere: the half of the earth's surface north of the equator.

oasis: a spot in a desert made fertile by the presence of water.

ocean: one of the large areas of the earth into which the water surface is divided.

orbit of the earth: the path of the earth as it revolves around the sun.

parallel: a latitude line running east and west around the earth parallel to the equator.

peak: the highest point of a mountain.

peninsula: a piece of land extending into the sea almost completely surrounded by water.

perihelion: the time of the year when the earth is closest to the sun.

plain: a flat or level area of land.

plateau: an elevated area of mostly level land, sometimes containing deep canyons.

population: the number of people or inhabitants living in a country, a city or town, or a particular area.

 # Mapping Skills

prime meridian: the zero meridian from which east and west longitude are measured, passing through London (Greenwich).

range: a group or chain of high elevations.

reef: a chain of coral rocks or ridge of sand lying at or near the surface of a body of water.

reservoir: a man-made lake where water is kept for future use.

revolution: the movement of the earth in its orbit around the sun, or the moon around the earth.

river: a large stream of water which flows on the earth's surface.

scale: the numerical relationship between an actual distance on the earth and the distance which represents it on a map.

sea: a large body of salt water smaller than an ocean.

sea level: the surface level of the oceans. It is the same all over the world.

seasons: the divisions of the year – spring, summer, autumn, winter – determined by the position of the earth in relation to the sun.

solstices: the times of the year, about June 21 and December 22, when the sun's rays reach their northern and southern limits at the tropic lines.

source: the place of origin of a river or stream.

south: the directions along a meridian toward the South Pole.

South Pole: the point farthest south on the earth's surface. It is 90° south of the equator.

southern hemisphere: the half of the earth's surface south of the equator.

symbol: a drawing, letter, or figure that represents a feature or idea.

strait: a narrow body of water connecting two larger bodies of water.

swamp: a low area of wet, spongy ground.

topographic map: a map that shows the detailed surface features, both natural and cultural, of a small area.

tributary: a river or stream that flows into a larger stream or other body of water.

Tropic of Cancer: an imaginary line of latitude 23° 30' north of the equator.

Tropic of Capricorn: an imaginary line of latitude 23° 30' south of the equator.

up: away from the center of the earth toward a point directly overhead.

valley: a long, narrow, land area lying between two areas of higher elevation. A valley usually contains a river or stream.

 # Mapping Skills

vegetation: all the different kinds of plant life that grow on the earth's surface.

volcano: a cone-shaped mountain that has an opening in the earth's crust from which lava can flow.

waterfall: a sudden drop of a stream from a high level to a much lower level.

water hemisphere: the hemisphere with the maximum water area, roughly centered at 40° S. latitude and 179° W. longitude.

west: the direction along a parallel toward the setting sun.

western hemisphere: the half of the earth that includes North America, South America and their waters.

year: the time required for one revolution of the earth around the sun.

Teacher Information

What is a Map?

A map is a drawn or printed representation of the earth or any other heavenly body. Most maps are flat, although some have raised surfaces. A *globe* is also a map in the shape of a sphere.

Maps provide information through lines, colors, shapes, and symbols. The symbols represent such features as rivers, lakes, roads, and cities. The features on a map are greatly reduced in size. The distance of 160 kilometers (100 miles) might be represented by 2.5 centimeters (1 inch) on a map.

Maps are used to locate places, measure distances, plan trips, and find our way. Pilots of ships and airplanes use maps to navigate. Maps provide us with information about a place, such as climate, population, and transportation routes. Some maps show such patterns as where people live and how they use the land.

Through the years, people have explored more of the world and have added new information to maps. Scientific discoveries have made maps more accurate. Today, most maps are based on photographs taken from the air. The making and study of maps is called *cartography*. The maker of a map, or someone who studies maps, is called a *cartographer*.

Types of Maps

There are many types of maps. The most common ones are *general reference maps, mobility maps,* thematic maps and *inventory maps.*

General reference maps identify and locate various geographic features. They may include land features, bodies of water, political boundaries, cities and towns, roads and many other elements. General reference maps are used to locate specific places and to observe their location in relation to other places. Examples of general reference maps are maps of provinces, states, countries, and continents. These maps are usually found in atlases.

Mapping Skills

A *political map* is one that emphasizes the boundaries of counties, provinces, states and countries. *Physical maps* or *terrain maps* emphasize the location of physical features found on the earth's surface such as mountains, rivers and lakes.

Mobility maps are created to help people find their way from one place to another. There are mobility maps for travel on land, on water, or in the air. Maps that are used to navigate ships and planes are called *charts*.

The most common mobility map is a *road map*. A road map represents different types of roads such as divided highways, four-lane roads, major routes and scenic routes. It also shows the location of cities, towns, provincial and state parks, and other places connected by these roads. Travelers use road maps to plan trips and to follow lengthy routes.

A *street map* is similar to a road map. It shows a much smaller area in much greater detail. This type of map is used to locate specific addresses and to plan and follow short routes.

Transit maps show the routes of buses, subways, and other systems of public transportation in cities and towns. These maps help people reach their destination by means of public transportation.

Aeronautical charts are maps used to navigate airplanes. Pilots of small, low-flying aircraft plan and follow a course by using *VFR charts* (visual flight rules charts). VFR charts show such landmarks as bridges, highways, railroad tracks, rivers and towns. These charts also show the location of airports, the heights of *mountains and other obstructions. Pilots of low-flying airplanes and crews of high-flying aircraft use IFR charts* (instrument flight rules charts). These charts are designed for radio navigation. IFR charts locate transmitters that beam very high radio frequency signals, which help pilots and airplane crews to determine their position and course.

Nautical charts are maps used to navigate ships and boats. They show the depths of water, the location of lighthouses, buoys, islands, and dangers such as coral reefs and underwater mountains that come close to the surface. Nautical charts also locate the source of radio signals that navigators use to determine their course and position.

Thematic Maps

A *thematic map* shows the distribution of a particular feature such as population, rainfall or a natural resource. This type of map is used to study an overall pattern. A thematic map may show where wheat is produced in North America or how the average rainfall varies from one part of a country to another. Quantities are expressed on thematic maps through the use of symbols or colors.

Inventory Maps

Inventory maps are similar to thematic maps in the way that they concentrate on a specific feature. These maps show the precise location of the specific feature. A map showing every building in a community is an example of an inventory map.

Mapping Skills

Reading a Map

In order to read a map, one must understand *map legends*, *scale*, *geographic grids* and *map indexes*.

A *map legend* lists and explains the symbols and colors found on a map. Sometimes the map symbols do resemble the features that they represent. For example, a tree-shaped symbol may represent a forest or an orchard. Many symbols have no resemblance to what they represent at all. For example a circle or large dot may represent where a city stands or it may represent where a group of homes can be found. It is very important to read the map legend to find out what the symbols mean. Most maps are printed to show north at the top. Most map legends include an arrow that indicates which direction is north.

Scale

The *scale* on a map shows the relationship between distances on the map and the corresponding distances on the earth's surface. Scale is shown on a straight line with distances marked off on a *bar scale*. A bar scale is like a ruler or measuring tape. You can measure long distances with a bar scale. Each mark represents a certain number of miles or kilometers.

Some maps indicate scale in words and figures. The scale might appear as 2.5 centimeters = 10 kilometers (1 inch = 6 miles). In other words 2.5 centimeters (1 inch) represents a distance of 10 kilometers (6 miles) on the earth's surface.

Geographic Grids

Geographic grids are lines on maps that help us find and describe locations. The most common grid uses the east-west lines, called *parallels*, and the north-south lines, called *meridians*. The parallel lines and the *meridians form the graticule.*

Parallels are lines that encircle the globe from *east* to *west*. The parallel that lies exactly halfway between the North and South Pole is called the *equator*. Parallels are used to measure *latitude*. They measure distance from the equator toward either pole. Latitude is measured in *degrees of a circle*. Any point on the equator has a latitude of zero degrees, written "0°". The North Pole has a latitude of 90° north and the South Pole has a latitude of 90° south. Parallels are sometimes called *lines of latitude*.

Meridians are lines that extend halfway around the globe from the North Pole to the South Pole. Mapmakers *count meridians from the line that passes through Greenwich, England, a borough of London. The* Greenwich meridian is also known as the *prime meridian*. Meridians measure longitude, which is the distance east or west of the prime meridian. *Longitude* is measured in degrees of a circle too. Meridians run from 0° at Greenwich to 180°. The 180° meridian lies halfway around the world from the Prime Meridian. Meridians are sometimes *called lines of longitude.*

Longitude and latitude are used to pinpoint places around the world.

Map Indexes

A *map index* helps us to locate places on a map. The features shown on a map are listed in alphabetical order in the index. At the back of most atlases, an index is found. Each entry in the index is listed with its longitude and latitude.

Mapping Skills

Some maps are divided into horizontal rows and vertical columns by an index grid. Letters are often used along the sides of the map to label the horizontal lines. Numbers are used across the top and bottom of the map to label the vertical rows. In this case, each entry in the map index is followed by a letter and a number corresponding to a row and a column on the map. This feature is found where the row and column cross.

Hemispheres

A *hemisphere* is one-half of a sphere. The word *hemisphere* is the name given to any half of the globe. It comes from the Greek word that means *half a sphere*. The world is divided into four main hemispheres. They are: 1) the northern and southern hemispheres, 2) the eastern and western hemispheres, 3) land and water hemispheres, and 4) daylight and darkness hemispheres.

The *northern and southern hemispheres* share the equator as a boundary line. All areas north of the equator make up the northern hemisphere. All areas south of the equator make up the southern hemisphere.

The *eastern and western hemispheres* have no natural dividing line such as the Equator. The eastern hemisphere, or "Old World", is made up of the continents of *Europe, Asia, Africa* and *Australia*. The western hemisphere, or "New World", is made up of the continents of *North America* and *South America*.

The earth is also divided as a *land hemisphere* and a *water hemisphere*. The land hemisphere includes half of the earth with the *most land*. Its center lies near London, England. The other half of the earth is mostly water and makes up the water hemisphere. Its center lies near New Zealand.

During a day, one half of the earth is in *darkness* and the other is in *light*. The earth is also separated into a *daylight* and *darkness hemispheres*. There is no sharp boundary between the daylight and darkness hemispheres. They are separated by the *twilight zones of dawn and dusk*. At the same time, they are continually changing their position on the surface of the earth as it rotates on its axis.

Directional Indicators

Most maps have a symbol called a *compass rose*. The purpose of the compass rose is to show the cardinal directions: *North, South, East, West*. Some compass roses have only four lines, called *petals*. Some directional indicators may only show "N" for North.

Sometimes a compass rose will have more than four directions. These are called the intermediate directions. The *intermediate petals* fall between two of the cardinal directions. They are called *northeast*, southeast, northwest, and *southwest*. One way to remember direction is with the word *"WE"*: West is on the left and East in on the right.

If a compass rose is not found on the map, the *top* of the map is usually *north*.

Map Symbols

One way to show features on a map is to create *symbols* that represent them. A symbol is a shape or pattern that represents an object. Symbols and their meanings are shown on a *key* or *legend* on the map.

Student Booklet
Mapping Skills Activities

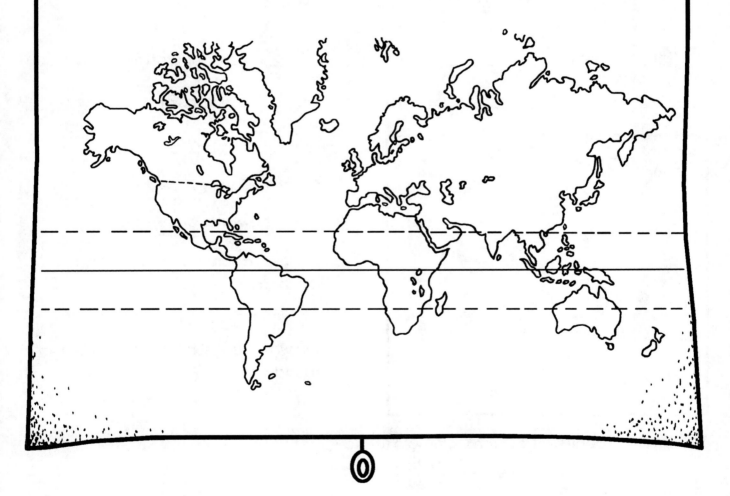

Name: _____

 # Mapping Skills

What is a Map?

Use the words in the box to complete the sentences which follow.

flat	roads	continent	map
buildings	trees	earth	picture
water	land	city	world
country	picture	diagram	

A _____ is like a _____ of the _____ taken from high up in the air or from space. A map is a _____ of a _____, _____, _____ or the _____.

Maps can show _____ and _____ areas found on the earth. Many things that are located upon the land areas such as _____, _____ and _____ are shown on maps. Most maps are _____.

This is a map of British Columbia.

1. Color the land *green*

2. Color the water *blue*.

3. In which country would you find British Columbia?

   _____

4. On which coast is British Columbia found?

   _____

5. In which continent is British Columbia found?

_____

6. Which land areas border British Columbia?

_____

_____

Mapping Skills

1. Why are maps important, and what are they used for?

   _____
   _____
   _____
   _____
   _____
   _____
   _____

2. What types of information can one gain from different types of maps of a country? Certain maps tell us:

   _____
   _____
   _____
   _____
   _____
   _____
   _____
   _____
   _____
   _____
   _____
   _____

3. What is cartography?

   _____
   _____

4. What is a cartographer?

   _____
   _____

Kinds of Maps

1. There are many types of maps used today and for a variety of reasons. The most common ones are:

   a) _____
   b) _____
   c) _____

Mapping Skills

General Reference Maps

2. General reference maps may show:

   a) _____

   b) _____

   c) _____

   d) _____

   Examples of general reference maps are:

   a) _____

   b) _____

   c) _____

   d) _____

3. Where are general reference maps found?

   _____

4. What is a political map?

   _____

   _____

5. What is a physical or relief map?

   _____

   _____

Mobility Maps

1. What is a mobility map?

   _____

   _____

2. How are mobility maps used?

   _____

   _____

3. What is a chart?

   _____

   _____

4. Who uses charts?

   _____

   _____

5. Which type of mobility map is the most common?

_____

_____

_____

6. What elements are found on a road map?

_____

_____

_____

7. Name other types of mobility maps.

_____   _____

_____   _____

_____   _____

Thematic Maps

1. What is a thematic map?

_____

_____

_____

Some types of thematic maps show:

_____   _____

_____   _____

_____   _____

Inventory Maps

1. What is an inventory map?

_____

_____

_____

Example:

_____

_____

_____

Mapping Skills

Directional Indicators

Part A:

A _____ is an instrument that shows which _____ we are facing or traveling. An ordinary compass is a _____, _____ box with a _____ inside it. The needle always points _____.

NORTH
WEST   EAST
SOUTH

In this drawing of a compass, the arrows point to these directions: _____, _____, _____ and _____. These directions are called _____ directions or the cardinal _____, of the compass.

Between each cardinal direction there is an _____ direction.

The intermediate directions are _____, _____, _____ and _____.

Complete the following activity.

a) On the drawing of the compass, mark a point on the circle about halfway between the words *north* and *east*. Draw a straight line from the center of the circle to that point. Label the point NE. Those letters stand for the word _____. It is the name of the direction halfway between _____ and _____.

b) Draw a straight line from the center of the circle to a point on the circle halfway between the words *south* and *east*. Label that point SE, the abbreviation for the word _____.

c) Draw a straight line from the center of the circle to a point halfway between the words *north* and *west*. Label it NW, which stands for _____.

d) Draw a straight line from the center of the circle to a point halfway between the words *south* and *west*. Label it SW, which stands for _____.

 # Mapping Skills

Compass Rose

Part B:

A _____ usually has a symbol called a _____ _____.

Below are some examples.

  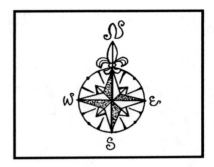

The purpose of the compass rose is to show the _____ directions: _____(N), _____(E), _____(S), _____(W).

Some compass roses just show N for _____. Directly below north is _____, to the right is _____ and to the left is _____.

Label the following compass rose by printing the cardinal and intermediate directions on it. Beside each abbreviation write the full word on the line.

1. N = _____
2. E = _____
3. SW = _____
4. NW = _____
5. SE = _____
6. NE = _____
7. S = _____
8. W = _____

If a compass rose is not on a map, the _____ of the map is usually _____.

 # Mapping Skills

Map Symbols

A _____ "stands for something". Mapmakers use small _____ or

symbols to stand for different things when they make their _____. The symbol

often looks like or suggests the feature it _____.

Example:

You can _____ recognize what each symbol represents.

Legend	
🏴	school
✝	church
🏠	house
🌳	tree
═══	highway
───	road

A map usually has a _____ or a

_____. A key is the _____ that

_____ the door to reading the map. The

symbols are contained in a _____.

Mapping Skills

Map Symbols Used in Atlases

The symbols below are ones frequently seen on most maps. Label each one neatly.

1. ─ ▪ ─ ─ ▪ ─ _____

2. ─ ▪ ─ ─ ▪ ─ _____

3. ⭐ _____

4. ◉ _____

5. ▪■▬ _____

6. _____

7. _____

8. ▲ _____

9.)(_____

10. _____

11. _____

12. _____

13. _____

14. └┴┴┴┴┘ _____

15. _____

16. _____

17. ●●● _____

18. _____

19. ⑤ _____

20. ╫╫╫╫╫╫╫ _____

A Map Tells Distance

A map can be used to tell distance when it has a _____ _____.

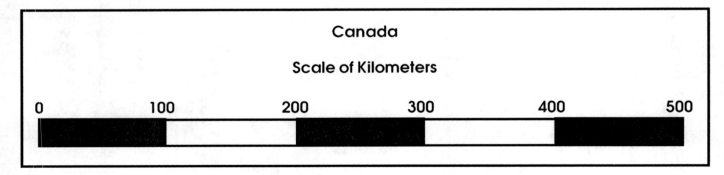

# Mapping Skills

A bar scale is like a _____ or _____. You can measure _____ distances with a bar scale.

What does "scale" mean?

_____

_____

Maps are _____ _____ or plans of places. A map of a country, a city, or even a room could be too _____ to use if it were drawn to exactly the same size as the place really is. Mapmakers let a small length such as a _____ stand for a _____ or a _____.

What is a Globe?

Use the words in the box to complete the following sentences about the globe.

shapes	lands	positions	stand	world
seas	triangular	earth	map	terrestrial
globe	sphere	gores	printed	spin
pasted	world map	roundness	rotates	

A _____ is a model of the _____. It shows the _____ of our _____. A globe is mounted on a _____ so that it can _____ showing how the earth _____ as it travels around the sun.

A globe is a _____ that has been _____ or _____ on a hollow _____. Globes of the earth are called _____ globes.

They are made of a series of _____ strips of material called _____. The gores are pasted on a sphere and a _____ is printed on the gores.

A globe shows all the _____ and _____ in their true _____ and _____.

Mapping Skills

How are Globes Used?

1. How are globes used?

_____

_____

2. Why is a globe important?

_____

_____

_____

Hemispheres

1. What is a hemisphere?

_____

_____

2. Into how many hemispheres is the globe divided?

_____

_____

3. What are the four hemispheres called?

_____   _____

_____   _____

The Northern and Southern Hemispheres

The northern and southern hemispheres share the _____ as a _____ line. All areas _____ of the equator make up the _____ hemisphere. All the areas _____ of the equator make up the _____ hemisphere.

A)

_____

_____

B)

_____

_____

Mapping Skills

The Eastern and Western Hemispheres

The eastern and western hemispheres do not have a _____ _____ _____. The eastern hemisphere is made up of the continents of _____, _____, _____ and _____. The western hemisphere is made up of the continents of _____ _____ and _____ _____.

A) _____
_____

B) _____
_____

Land and Water Hemispheres

The land hemisphere includes the _____ of the earth with the _____ land. Its center lies near _____, _____. The other half of the earth is mainly _____. This makes up the _____ _____. Its center lies near _____.

Daylight and Darkness Hemispheres

During one day, one half of the earth is in _____ and one half is in _____. There is no definite _____ _____ between the daylight and darkness hemispheres. These hemispheres are separated by the _____ zones of _____ and _____. These hemispheres are continually changing positions on the earth's surface as it _____ on its axis.

Lines on the Globe

_____ are _____ on maps that help us _____ and describe locations.

The most common grid uses the east-west lines called _____ of _____ and the north-south lines called _____ or _____ of _____.

Mapping Skills

Each parallel of latitude runs _____ to _____ and describes the position of a point on the earth's surface in relation to the _____.

The latitude of a point is measured in _____ from the equator towards one of the _____ _____.

The _____ has a latitude of _____ _____ (written 0⁰). The North Pole has a latitude of _____ _____ and the South Pole has a latitude of _____ _____. _____ of latitude are divided into _____ minutes (') and the minutes each consist of 60 seconds (").

Lines of _____ or _____ begin in _____, a borough of London. Greenwich lies at 0⁰ longitude. This line of longitude is called the _____ _____. Lines of longitude are lines that run from the _____ to _____ on maps and globes to indicate distances and locate points. All the lines of longitude _____ at the North and South Poles. The distance between the meridians is greatest at the equator. This distance gradually _____ as the meridians (lines of longitude) near the poles.

Label the following parallels of latitude on the globe.

| Tropic of Cancer | Arctic Circle | North Pole | Equator |
| Tropic of Capricorn | Antartic Circle | South Pole | |

Parallels of Latitude

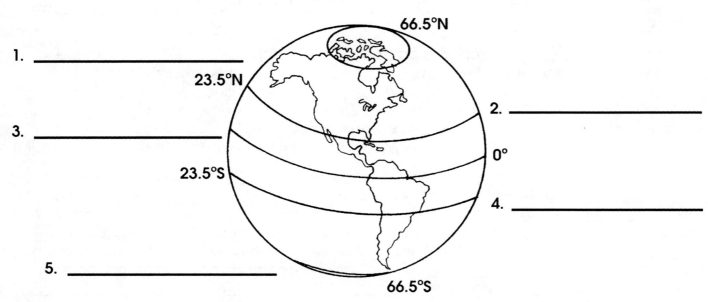

1. _____

2. _____

3. _____

4. _____

5. _____

Mapping Skills

Day and Night

A _____ day is the length of time that it takes the _____ to turn around once with respect to the sun. _____ refers to the time when the _____ is shining on our part of the earth. _____ refers to the time when our part of the earth is _____ or turned _____ from the sun.

Each day begins at _____ in most countries and the day is divided into _____ parts of _____ hours each. The hours from _____ to _____ are the _____ (before noon) hours. The hours from _____ to _____ are the _____ (after noon) hours.

The length of _____ changes during the year in all parts of the world. The _____ of the earth's _____ causes one _____ to _____ towards the sun and the other to slant away from the sun. When the earth's axis causes the _____ Pole to face the sun, the _____ Pole is continuously _____. As the North Pole tilts _____ from the sun, it becomes _____ while the South Pole has constant _____.

The Seasons

Each year the earth goes through _____ seasons. The seasons are _____, _____, _____ and _____. Each season lasts approximately _____ months and brings changes in _____, _____ and the _____.

During the spring, the days are _____ and get _____. Summers can be _____ during the day and _____ at night. In the autumn, days become _____ and begin to _____. During the winter it is _____ with much _____ days.

The _____ seasons are caused by the changing _____ of the earth in relation to the sun. When the _____ slants towards the sun, the _____ hemisphere receives the _____ sunlight and it is summer. When the North Pole slants away from the sun, the northern hemisphere receives the _____ sunlight and it is _____. Spring begins when the North Pole _____ to slant toward the sun and _____ begins when the North Pole starts to slant away again.

Summer begins in the northern hemisphere on _____ during the summer _____. The sun is high in the sky and this is the _____ day of the year. The _____ solstice marks the beginning of winter on _____ and this day is the _____ one of the year. The Vernal Equinox marks the beginning of _____ on _____. The Autumnal Equinox is the beginning of autumn which takes place on _____ or _____. During each equinox, places on the earth have approximately _____ hours of _____ and _____ hours of _____.

Mapping Skills

Basic Mapping Skills Card #1

Using a Directional Indicator

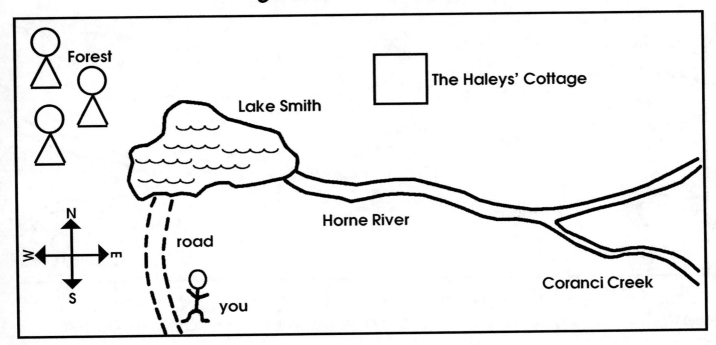

Maps give you a lot of information.

On this map there is a special symbol **N**. It is called a **directional indicator**. This symbol shows us where **north** is.

If **you** walk along the road, you are heading **north** and will soon be at Lake Smith.

Color Lake Smith, Horne River and Coranci Creek **blue**.

Color the road **brown**.

Color the Haleys' Cottage **yellow**.

Color the forest **green**.

Go over the directional indicator in **red**.

Mapping Skills

Basic Mapping Skills Card #2

Using a Directional Indicator

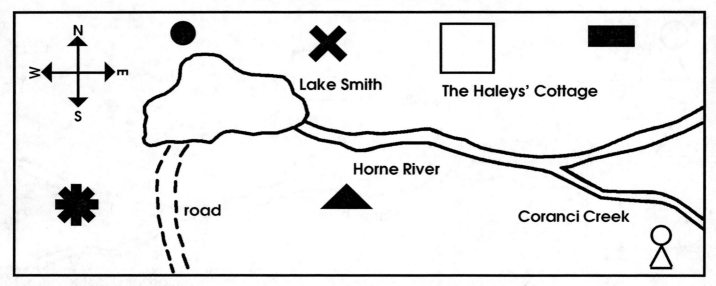

Some maps give a directional indicator showing north, south, east and west. This will help you to locate a place on the map and it will also tell someone else how to find it.

Example: "The Haleys' cottage is north of Horne River."
"The road is south of Lake Smith."

On the map are some symbols:

Complete these sentences using the words **north**, **south**, **west** or **east**.

1. The ✖ is _____ of the Haleys' cottage.
2. The ▬ is _____ of the Haley's cottage.
3. The ▲ is _____ of Horne River.
4. The ♟ is _____ of Coranci River.
5. The ● is _____ of Smith Lake.
6. The ✳ is _____ of the _____ .

Mapping Skills

Basic Mapping Skills Card #3

Reading a Map

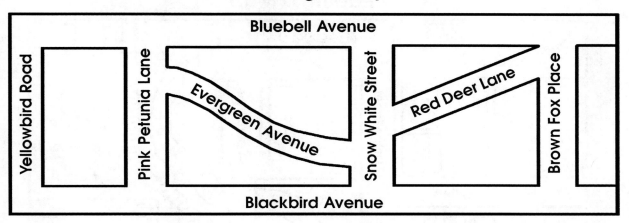

Color each street the color that is part of its name.

Mapping Skills

Basic Mapping Skills Card #4

Reading a Map

Fill in the right direction.

North, South, East, West

1. Spirit Town is _____ of Ghost Town.

2. Dragon City is _____ of Ghost Town.

3. Monster Village is _____ of _____ and _____.

4. Gremlin City is _____ of Spirit Town.

5. Spirit Town is _____ of Gremlin City.

Mapping Skills

Basic Mapping Skills Card #5

Reading a Map

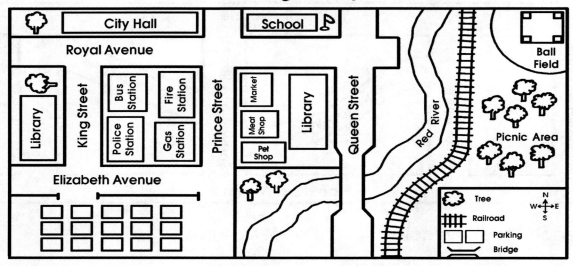

Complete each sentence below with the correct answer.

1. The ball field is _____ of the picnic area.

2. The school is found at the corner of _____ Street and _____ Street.

3. City Hall is located on _____.

4. Parking is available south of _____.

5. The railroad runs _____ and _____ and is located _____ of the Red River.

6. The _____ is found on Queen Street.

7. City Hall is located on _____.

8. Royal Avenue runs _____ and _____.

9. On Prince Street, you can shop for food at the _____ and the _____.

10. You can catch a bus at the corner of _____ Street and _____ Avenue.

Mapping Skills

Basic Mapping Skills Card #6

Map Symbols

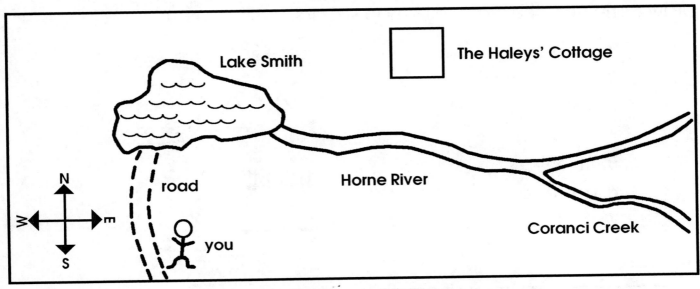

On the map above there are symbols that represent different features on it.

What does each symbol represent?

1. ☐ means _____

2. 🗺 means _____

3. 〰 means _____

4. ·----- means _____

On the map above draw three trees west of the Haleys' cottage.

On the map above draw two trees south of the Horne River.

This symbol ooooooooooooooo will represent a path.

Make a path from the Haleys' cottage to the lake.

Color your map.

Mapping Skills

Basic Mapping Skills Card #7

Recognizing Map Symbols

Draw a line from the word to its map symbol.

1. bridge
2. mountains
3. lake
4. boundary line
5. river
6. railroad
7. highway
8. city

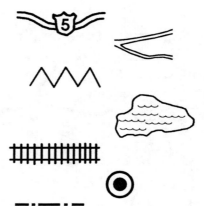

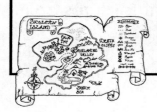

Mapping Skills

Basic Mapping Skills Card #8

Using Map Symbols to Make a Map

On a large sheet of paper draw a map using these symbols.

Remember to put on a directional indicator.

 lake    forest   house   river

 church   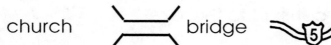 bridge   road    railroad

Mapping Skills

Basic Mapping Skills Card #9

The Legend or Key

Legend

lake

river

cottage

road

path

tree

Most maps have a legend or key that helps you to read the map correctly.

Since the space on a map is limited, symbols are used instead of words.

The symbols are listed in a "legend" or "key".

The legend or key unlocks the code and tells you what the symbols represent.

Each symbol in a legend must match the color and shape of the symbol used on a map.

Color the legend's symbols.

Then color the same symbols on the map to match.

Mapping Skills

Basic Mapping Skills Card #10

Making a Map

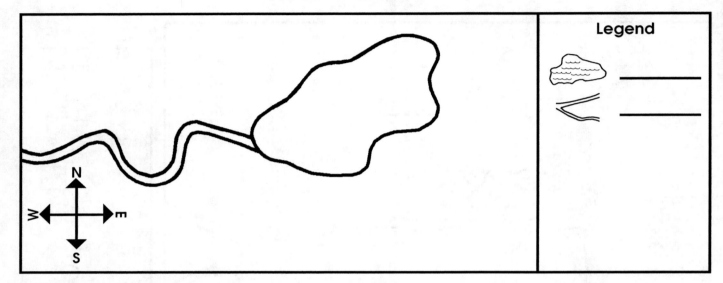

Above is a picture of Marty's Lake. Karen Creek runs into Marty's Lake.

Follow the directions below and complete the map and the legend.

1. Be sure to print in pencil.

2. Make symbols to match the underlined words in the information below. Put the symbols on the legend. Color each symbol.

   • Beth and Sandra live south of Marty's Lake in a **house**.
   • Bruce and Mike live in a **house** south of Karen Creek but right by the creek.
   • There is a **road** from Beth and Sandra's house to Bruce and Mike's house.
   • South of Beth and Sandra's house is a **school**.
   • North of the lake is a **store**.
   • There are **two trees** east of Bruce and Mike's house.

3. Place the symbols on the map to match the information given in the legend.

4. Color the symbols on the map to match those on the legend.

Mapping Skills

Basic Mapping Skills Card #11

Mapping Your Class!

List the things that you must remember to show when you make a map.

1. _____
2. _____
3. _____
4. _____

In the rectangle below, make a map of your classroom area. Don't forget to make a legend to show what each symbol means. **Color** your map carefully and **print** very neatly.

Map of My Classroom

	Legend

Mapping Skills

Basic Mapping Skills Card #12

Mapping My School Grounds

This is a map of Owain and Erich's school grounds. It shows us where the road, the playing field, the creek and the "climbers" are.

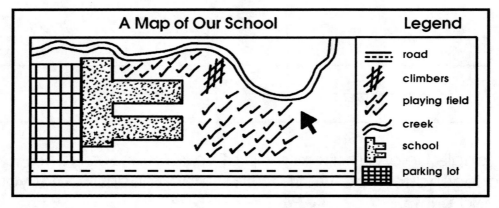

Make a map of your school grounds. Be sure to show the shape of your school.

Use symbols to represent things such as swings, playground equipment, the baseball diamond, climbers, basketball hoops, parking lot, playing field, etc.

Remember to:

1. Include a directional indicator and a legend.
2. Color your legend symbols and map symbols the same colors.
3. Use a pencil to draw your map and label it.

My School Grounds

	Legend

Mapping Skills

Basic Mapping Skills Card #13

Mapping Your Route to School

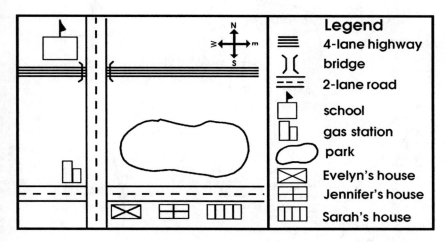

Legend
4-lane highway
bridge
2-lane road
school
gas station
park
Evelyn's house
Jennifer's house
Sarah's house

Evelyn, Jennifer and Sarah made a map of the route their bus takes to school each day.

They showed landmarks that would help someone to find his or her way and not get lost!

Landmarks are usually big buildings, parks, etc. that are easily noticed.

The girls only used a few symbols because they did not want to put too much information on the map. They showed only their homes.

Draw a map showing the best way to get from your house to the school. Only put on meaningful symbols.

Remember: 1. directional indicator   **2.** legend
            3. use a pencil   **4.** symbols must match in color

My Route to School

	Legend

Mapping Skills

Basic Mapping Skills Card #14

Using a Scale to Find Distance

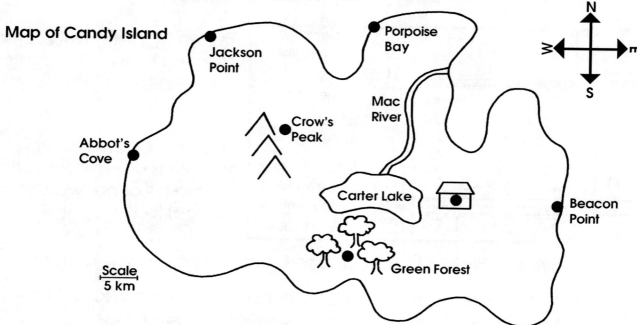

- The map of Candy Island has been "drawn to scale".

- On this map, drawing to scale means that one centimeter (cm) on the map equals five real kilometers (km).

- With a ruler, measure the distance from Abbot's Cove to Beacon Point. It is _____ cm long. Now multiply by five to find its distance in kilometers. The distance from Abbot's Cove to Beacon Point is _____ km.

Measure to find out the distances in kilometers

1. The distance from Crow's Peak to the house on Carter Lake is approximately _____ km.

2. From Porpoise Bay to Beacon Point is _____ km.

3. From Jackson Point to Porpoise Bay and then to the Green Forest is a total of _____ km.

4. To get from the Green Forest to Abbot's Cove by way of Crow's Peak is _____ km.

5. Using string, find the approximate distance all around Candy Island: _____ km.

Mapping Skills

Basic Mapping Skills Card #15

Using Scale to Find Distance

Use the scale to find the distance in kilometers.

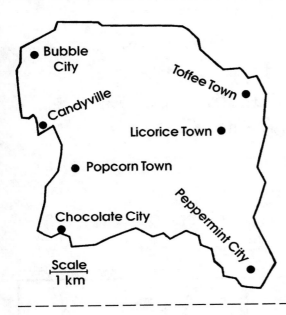

Scale
1 km

1. Bubble City to Candyville _____ km

2. Candyville to Toffee Town _____ km

3. Bubble City to Peppermint City _____ km

4. Popcorn Town to Peppermint City _____ km

5. Toffee Town to Chocolate City _____ km

6. Candyville to Licorice Town _____ km

- -

Basic Mapping Skills Card #16

Drawing to Scale

Draw a rectangle that is six meters long and four meters wide using the scale below.

Draw a square that is six meters on each side using the scale below.

```
0   1   2   3   4   5   6   7   8
|   |   |   |   |   |   |   |   |
        1 cm = 1 meter
```

```
0   1   2   3   4   5   6   7   8
|   |   |   |   |   |   |   |   |
        1 cm = 1 meter
```

Mapping Skills

Basic Mapping Skills Card #17

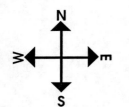

N-North
E-East
S-South
W-West

Using a Grid

Follow the instructions carefully.

1. From point A, draw a line north five spaces.
2. Travel east four spaces.
3. Go north three spaces.
4. Head east seven spaces.
5. Turn south three spaces.
6. Travel east four spaces.
7. Go south five spaces.
8. Travel west fifteen spaces.

Make a funny face out of your shape.

A

Mapping Skills

Basic Mapping Skills Card #18

Using Coordinates

Color the boxes:

A1 - Red
B2 - Black
D2 - Orange
C2 - Purple
A2 - Brown
C1 - Green
D1 - Yellow
B1 - Blue

	A	B	C	D
1				
2				

Mapping Skills

Basic Mapping Skills Card #19

Using Coordinates on a Grid

Draw a line between these points:

J 1 - B1	J1 - J10	H15 - H23	D23 - H23	A18 - 120
B 1 - B10	J1 - B10	H15 - D15	D15 - H23	A20 - D23
B10 - J10	B1 - J10	D15 - D23	D15 - A18	D15 - H23
				H15 - D23

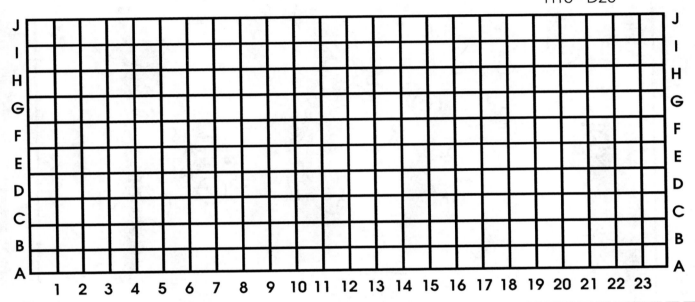

Basic Mapping Skills Card #20

Mapping to Scale

Carefully measure your classroom in meters or feet.

You are going to map your classroom to scale. You will work with a classmate.

Decide what your scale will be.

Example: 1 centimeter (cm) = 1 meter (m) or 1 inch (in) = 1 foot (ft)

Use one-centimeter or one-inch graph paper to help you plan the map. Show as many pieces of furniture (in scale) as you can.

Remember to measure carefully and do your map in pencil so it can be easily erased if you make a mistake.

Don't forget your legend, the symbols and the title.

Mapping Skills

World Mapping Skills Card #1

Our World

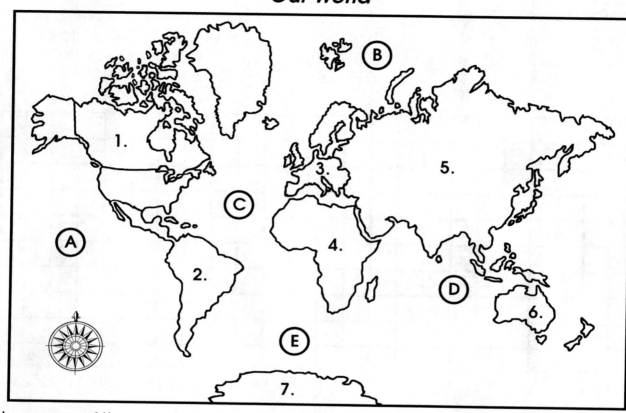

This is a map of the _____.

The world is divided into seven _____.

The continents are:

1. _____   5. _____
2. _____   6. _____
3. _____   7. _____
4. _____

Color each continent a different color.

In the world there are five _____.

The oceans are:

a) _____   d) _____

b) _____   e) _____

c) _____

Color the waters blue.

Mapping Skills

World Mapping Skills Card #2

Where Do We Live?

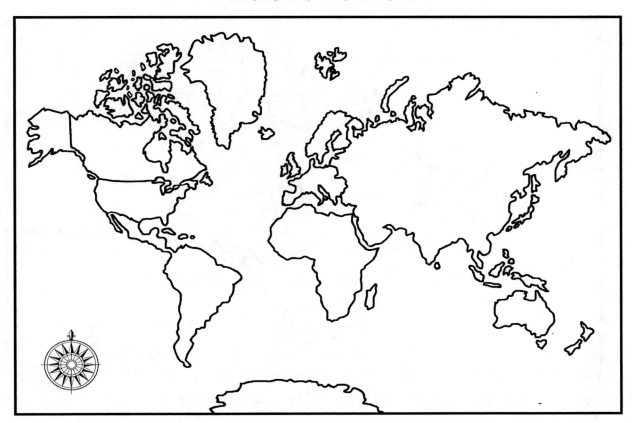

We live in the country called _____. It is located on the

continent called _____. There are _____

countries in North America. They are _____, the

_____ and _____.

On the east coast is found the _____. On the west coast

is found the _____.

Color Canada red, the United States yellow, and Mexico green.

The continent of North America is found in the _____.

Mapping Skills

World Mapping Skills Card #3

Reading the Map of North America

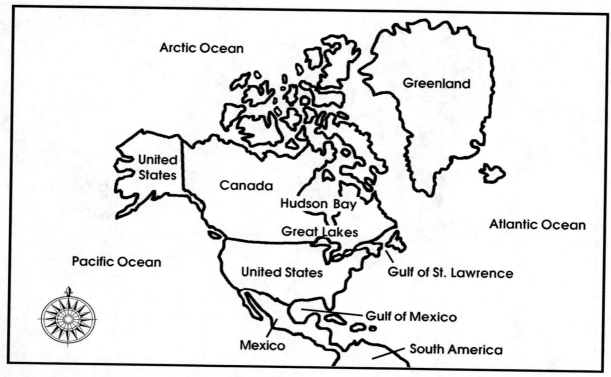

Complete the following sentences by choosing words from the map.

1. The continent shown on the map is _____.

2. The ocean east of North America is the _____.

3. The ocean north of North America is the _____.

4. The ocean west of North America is the _____.

5. _____ is the largest island.

6. Most of the islands in the north belong to _____.

7. The Great Lakes are part of the boundary between _____ and the _____.

8. The country of _____ is found south of the United States.

9. The Gulf of St. Lawrence and the Gulf of Mexico are two large bodies of _____ _____.

10. Hudson Bay reaches into the country of _____.

Mapping Skills

World Mapping Skills Card #4

Reading the Map of Canada

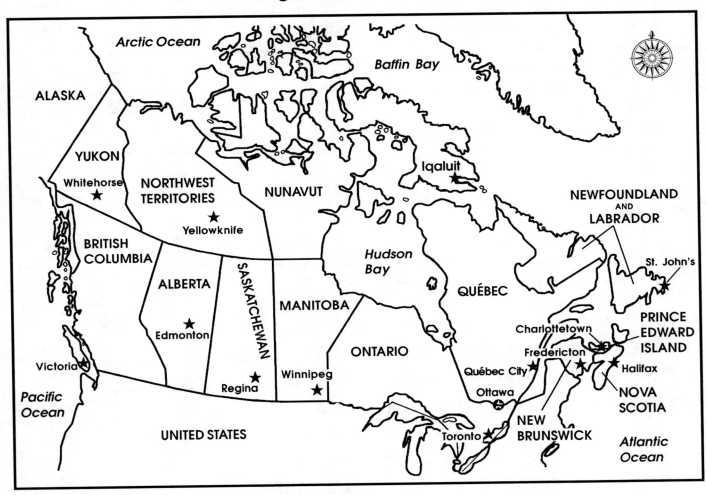

This is a _____ map of Canada. A political map shows
_____ and _____ between the _____,
_____, _____, and _____.

1. List the names of Canada's ten provinces and three territories in column A.
   List their capital cities in column B.

   Column A   **Column B**

   _____   _____

   _____   _____

Mapping Skills

_____   _____
_____   _____
_____   _____
_____   _____
_____   _____
_____   _____
_____   _____
_____   _____
_____   _____
_____   _____

2. Which five areas in Canada do not share any of their border with the United States?

    _____
    _____
    _____

3. Which body of water lies directly north of Canada? _____ west of Canada? _____ east of Canada? _____

4. Which area in Canada has the most islands? _____

5. What is the name of Canada's closest neighbor? _____

6. What is the name of the capital city of Canada? _____ In which province is it located? _____

7. Which province is an island? _____

8. Which province is an island and part of the mainland? _____

9. Which two provinces do not have any water as a border or boundary?

    _____

10. Which American state is west of the Yukon? _____

11. Which provincial capital city is located on an island in western Canada? _____ In which province is it found? _____

12. What are the names of the three prairie provinces?

    _____

13. What are the names of the atlantic provinces? _____

    _____

Mapping Skills

World Mapping Skills Card #5

Reading a Map of the United States

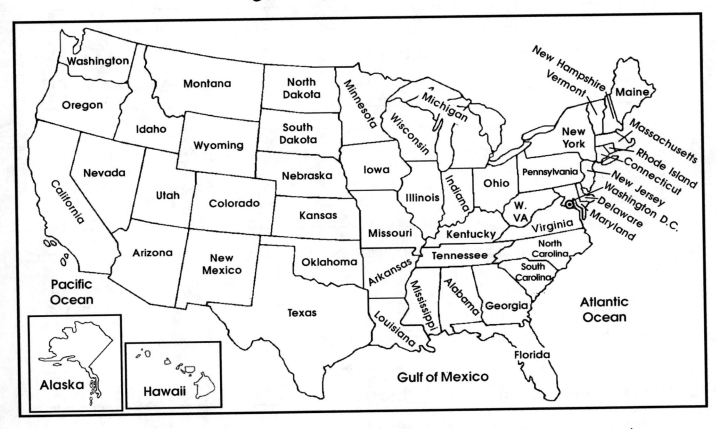

Look at the map of the United States carefully. Locate the answers to complete the sentences or to answer the questions that refer to this map.

1. The United States is also located in the continent of _____.

2. It is located between the countries of _____ and _____.

3. The United States is made up of _____ states and the District of Columbia.

4. What are the names of the states located on the west coast of the United States?

_____

 OTM-119 • SSA1-19 Mapping Activities & Outlines

Mapping Skills

5. What are the names of the states that border on the Gulf of Mexico?

_____

_____

6. Which states border the country of Canada?

_____

_____

_____

7. What are the names of the three rivers that are tributaries of the Mississippi River?

_____

_____

8. Which river forms part of the boundary between the United States and Mexico?

_____

9. Which two states are not connected to the United States physically?

_____

10. Which state is located the farthest south? _____

11. Which state is the farthest north? _____

12. Which two states are separated by one of the Great Lakes?

_____

13. What is the name of the capital city of the United States? _____

14. Which state is a long peninsula? _____

15. Which state is made up of a group of islands that vary in size and shape? _____

16. Make a list of the names of the states that you have visited.

_____

_____

Mapping Skills

World Mapping Skills Card #6

Labeling a Map

1. Obtain a map of the world from your teacher.

2. Using an atlas locate your country on a world map. Color it **green** on your world map.

3. Put a directional indicator on the map.

4. Locate the following oceans and neatly print their names on your world map.

    Atlantic Ocean   Indian Ocean
    Pacific Ocean   Southern Ocean
    Arctic Ocean

5. Choose the names of **ten** countries that you have heard about. Make a list of their names on the lines below.

    _____

    _____

    _____

    Now locate them on a world map. Label them neatly on the map. Be sure to print their names.

6. Which of those ten countries is the closest to your country?

    _____

7. Which of those ten countries are the farthest away?

    _____

8. How would you color your map? What color would the land be? What color will you make the the water?

    Discuss with your teacher and decide which colors you will need.

    Do you need a legend?

    What symbols will you use in your legend and on the map?

    Be sure to label your map neatly.

 # Mapping Skills

World Mapping Skills Card #7

Locating Places on a Map

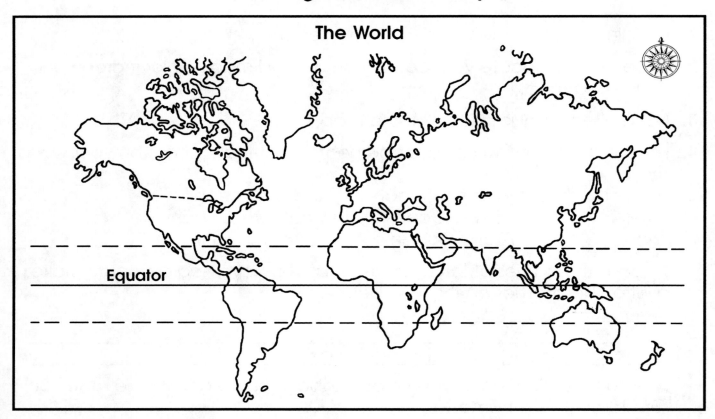

The World

Equator

Since the world map shows so many places, it is not always easy to locate something using only a directional indicator.

Cartographers decided a long time ago to use **imaginary** lines to help people when they read maps of the world.

On the map above, you will see three lines drawn across the world map. The center, solid line, is called the **equator**. It divides the world in half.

Countries above the equator are said to be "north of the equator", while countries below the equator are said to be "south of the equator".

Using an atlas and the world map above, complete the activities on the accompanying page.

 # Mapping Skills

1. Two countries that are **north** of the equator are _____ and _____.

2. Three countries that are **south** of the equator are _____, _____ and _____.

3. Name two countries that "touch" or lie along the equator. _____ and _____

4. The equator passes over three, large oceans. They are the _____, the _____ and the _____.

5. If a plane flew from Australia to Mexico, it would go over the equator. **True** or **False**

6. The equator passes over India. **True** or **False**

7. There are two broken lines shown on this world map. One lies north of the equator and the other lies to the south. Their names are the _____ and the _____.

8. Print their names on the broken lines in blue pencil.

9. Canada is found _____ of the Tropic of Cancer.

10. The Tropic of Capricorn passes through three continents. What are their names?
    _____
    _____

11. Australia is located _____ of the equator.

12. What are the names of the four continents that are north of the Tropic of Cancer?
    _____
    _____

Mapping Skills

World Mapping Skills Card #8

Locating Places on a Map

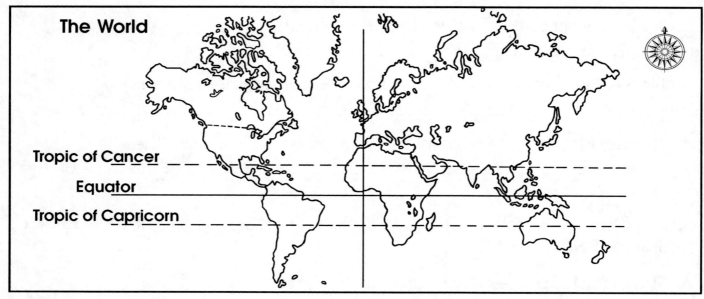

The World

Tropic of Cancer

Equator

Tropic of Capricorn

In order to make maps even easier to read, cartographers decided to put another imaginary line on the map of the world. This line has a special name. It is called the **prime meridian**.

All places in the world are either east or west of the prime meridian.

Print the word prime meridian in green along the line on the map.

Complete the following activities using the map.

1. Three countries that are east of the prime meridian are _____, _____ and _____.

2. Two countries that are west of the prime meridian are _____ and _____.

3. Name two countries that are north of the equator and east of the prime meridian. _____

4. Name two countries that are south of the equator and west of the prime meridian. _____

5. Australia is _____ of the equator and _____ of the prime meridian.

6. Mexico is _____ of the equator and _____ of the prime meridian.

Mapping Skills

World Mapping Skills Card #9

Locating Countries Using Coordinates

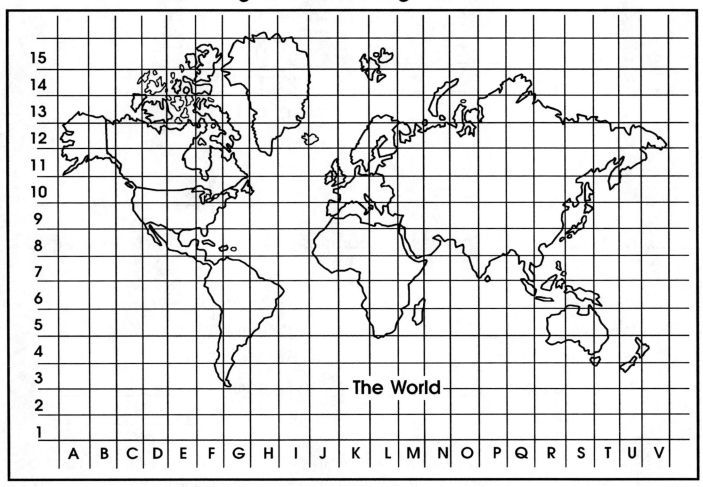

The World

Another way to locate countries or bodies of water is to divide up the world map as you see above. This is called a **grid**.

Put your finger on the letter **S** and move it up until it rests across from the number **5**.

Your finger is resting on Australia. That part of Australia is located at the coordinates of **S,5**.

Using this map, and a map of countries, locate land and/or bodies of water to answer the activities on the following page.

Mapping Skills

1. Use the coordinates below to locate a country or a body of water. Print its name on the line beside the coordinates.

   a) H,13 _____

   b) P,11 _____

   c) E,11 _____

   d) D,9 _____

   e) 0,6 _____

   f) U,4 _____

   g) H,6 _____

   h) 1,9 _____

   i) C,4 _____

   j) M,14 _____

   k) E,8 _____

   l) S,5 _____

2. Listed below are the names of countries found on a world map. Beside each one write the coordinates.

   a) Egypt _____

   b) France _____

   c) United States _____

   d) Canada _____

   e) India _____

   f) Mexico _____

   g) British Isles _____

   h) Africa _____

   i) Japan _____

   k) China _____

3. Although this method of locating countries or bodies of water is a good one, what problems might one have in using this method?

   _____

   _____

   _____

   _____

   _____

   _____

   _____

   _____

   _____

Mapping Skills

World Mapping Skills Card #10

Using Latitude and Longitude

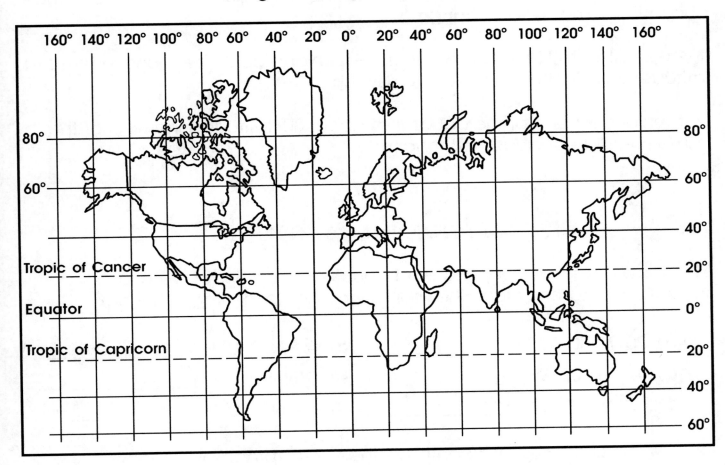

This is a map of the world that you would usually see in a student atlas.

It has the equator, Tropic of Cancer, Tropic of Capricorn and the prime meridian marked on it.

In addition, it also has other lines as well.

The lines that run the same way as the equator are called **parallels of latitude**.

The lines that run the same direction as the prime meridian are called **meridians of longitude**.

We usually call these lines just **latitude** and **longitude**.

 # Mapping Skills

All atlases are marked exactly the same way. The positions of the longitude and latitude lines **never change**.

If you wanted to tell someone where Greenland could be found in terms of latitude and longitude, you could say this:

"Greenland is north of the equator at about 80^0 latitude, and west of the prime meridian at about 40^0 longitude."

Or

you could just say, "80^0 N, 40^0 W".

1. Below are some coordinates of countries or bodies of water using latitude and longitude. Use your school atlas to identify each one.

   a) 20^0 N, 40^0 W _____
   d) 60^0 N, 140^0 E _____

   b) 40^0 N, 100^0 W _____
   e) 0^0 N, 80^0 E _____

   c) 60^0 N, 80^0 E _____
   f) 60^0 N, 100^0 W _____

2. Countries are big and can have their area spread over many coordinates. Write the coordinates in latitude and longitude that you think are proper for these countries.

   a) Australia _____
   d) France _____

   b) China _____
   e) Iceland _____

   c) Mexico _____
   f) New Zealand _____

Mapping Skills

Mapping Word Study Card #1

Look for the Worldly Words

Find the words in the word search map that pertain to mapping terms.

Circle each one that you are able to locate.

```
A M D Y Q A H D J W A Q F V P Q E A B Z O P Q Y I J
O I C O N T I N E N T S X P M O U N O M C R F H P G
K B O Z E N W I Q E Y G L T T R N D L A T I T U D E
N T M L F B R C U H R B K Z L S M D E N W M L X U K
R G P V H F G Y A K I J S T U C V G L O B E R V S W
O W A N O F O R T T K Y H R X I C Z R F B M A P V M
C Z S C C B L N O R T H P O L E S J A Q G E N W T X
I D S V E U S A R G Q Z J P I D H T E K Y R L P O U
R A R B A C A D P R C P P I T O A E Z R J I P G O H
P C O U N T R I E S Q J B C N B Y W L F Q D B M I K
A A S V S E C F E D U O S O U T H P O L E I L J F W
C R E N U W T I M F I K S F R A X G N S C A Y L N M
F D X L G A I D G G N S Q C U W M D G H D N E K N X
O I Q T C H C K E J H V L A X I S I I J B I X P V O
C N R J Z B C I L F H V T N Y Z L X T Q S W U Z D A
I A A R C T I C K B I H Q C F N U I U V K C U H Y E
P L D Z Q G R I D J G T R E O C G W D L R P A V C Z
O V F U L S C L O D N E R R S J T V E X M S W L F A
R I G N X P L E M P F Q S P D A H M X U T Q R G E A
T M W K O H E M I S P H E R E Z K Y L N T O Y S Z B
```

compass rose	continents	grid	North Pole
Tropic of Cancer	countries	oceans	Arctic Circle
Tropic of Capricorn	hemisphere	map	South Pole
prime meridian	longitude	axis	latitude
cardinal	scale	globe	equator

Mapping Skills

Mapping Word Study Card #2

Land Form Crossword Fun!

In the world there are many land forms. Read each crossword puzzle clue carefully and complete the puzzle.

Across:

2. an area of land completely surrounded by water
4. an unusually high elevation that rises steeply
6. the land bordering the sea
7. a body of fresh water
10. a large stream of fresh water
11. a long, narrow land area that lies between two mountains or hills
12. an arm of an ocean, sea or lake extending into land

Down:

1. a large, treeless, flat land
2. a narrow strip of land between two bodies of water, connecting two large land areas
3. a narrow, man-made waterway used by boats
5. a river or stream that flows into a larger stream or other body of water
8. a narrow body of water connecting two larger bodies of water
9. a triangular area of soil at the mouth of a river

Outline Maps of the World

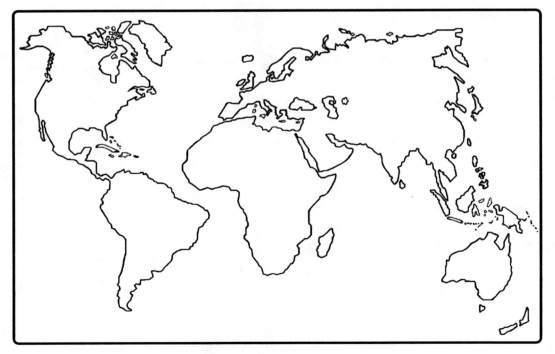

To the Teacher

Help students learn about many of the countries in our world. This resource can be used as a supplement with your existing social studies program. Reference material including atlases and encyclopedias will be needed for students to complete these pages.

Use the outline maps to:

- Teach the names and locations of countries, states and capital cities.

- Identify the physical characteristics such as vegetation zones, precipitation, temperature, soil types, landforms, natural resources for countries, states and provinces.

- Identify the major rivers and lakes of a country.

- Study the cultural characteristics, such as major economic activities, population density, and distribution of major religions, transportation routes, and ethnic origins.

- Research the historical political boundaries, battle sites, important historical events and migration routes.

- Discuss current events.

- Teach or review specific facts taught in your current program.

- Have students complete reports on countries of study.

- Have students create their own atlas, by using a number of maps in this resource.

- Make overhead transparencies.

- Create bulletin boards.

- Create puzzles or games.

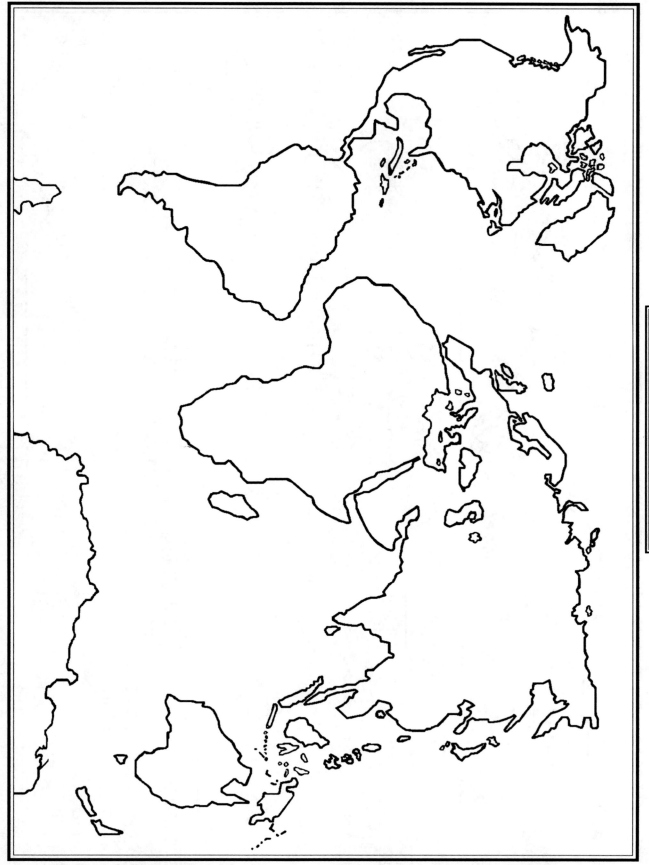

The World

The World

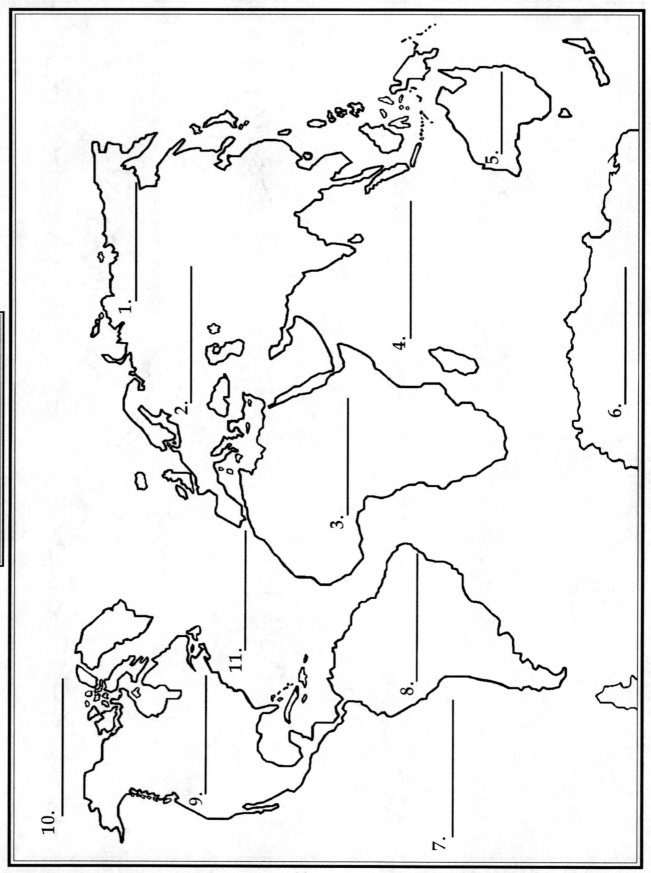

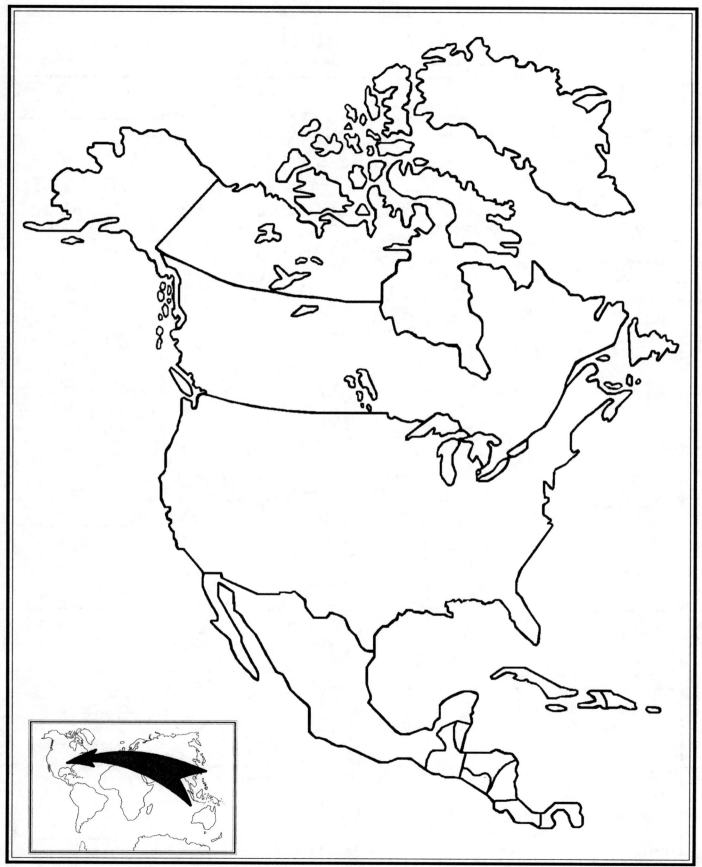

North America

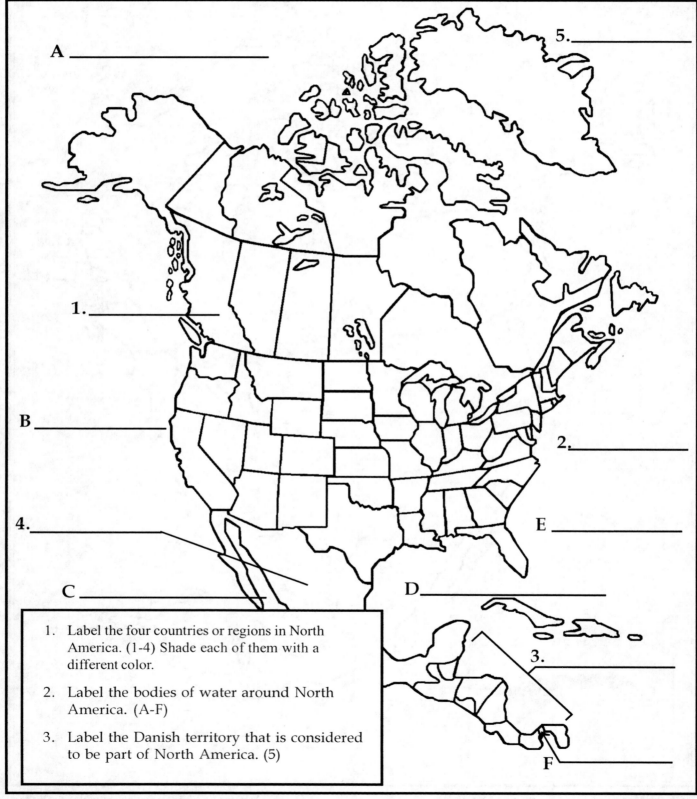

A _____

5. _____

1. _____

B _____

2. _____

4. _____

E _____

C _____

D _____

3. _____

F _____

1. Label the four countries or regions in North America. (1-4) Shade each of them with a different color.

2. Label the bodies of water around North America. (A-F)

3. Label the Danish territory that is considered to be part of North America. (5)

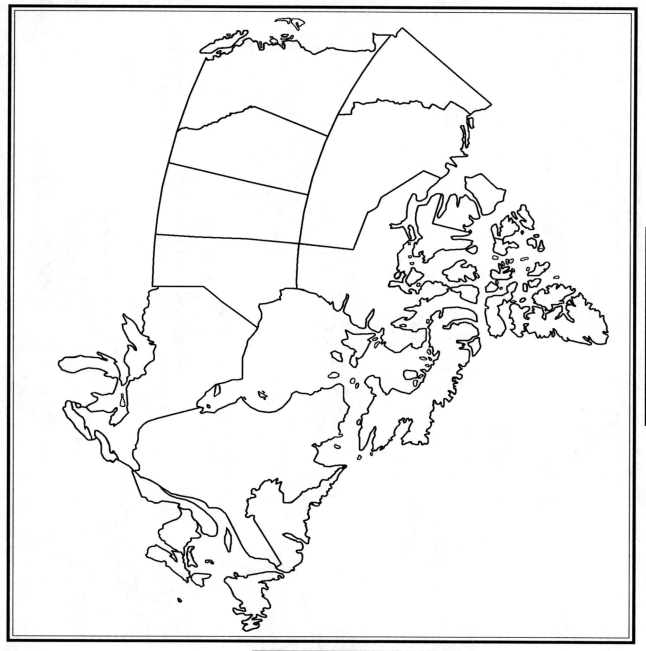

Canada

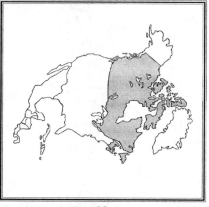

Canada

1. Label the 10 provinces and 3 territories.

2. Label these bodies of water: Beaufort Sea, Pacific Ocean, Hudson Bay, Atlantic Ocean and Baffin Bay.

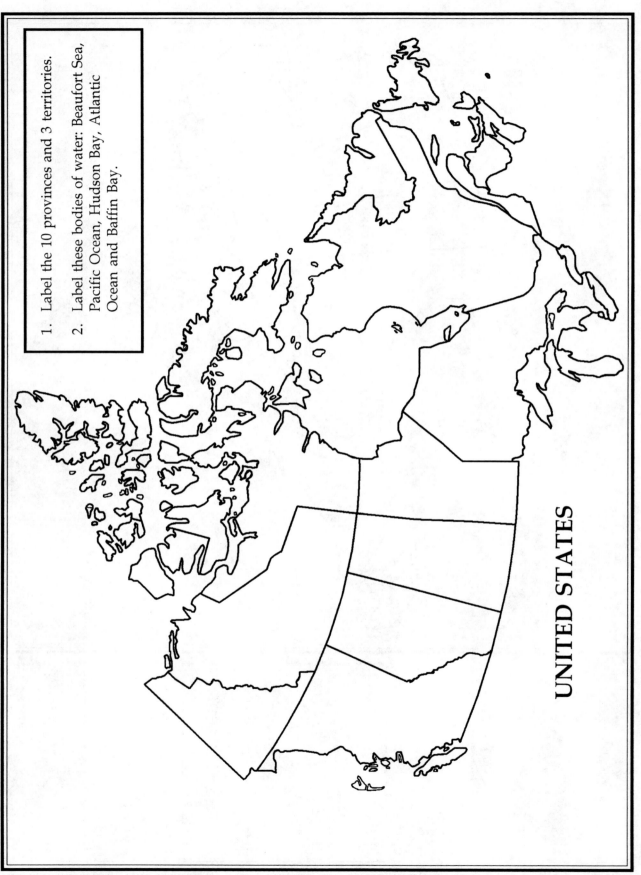

UNITED STATES

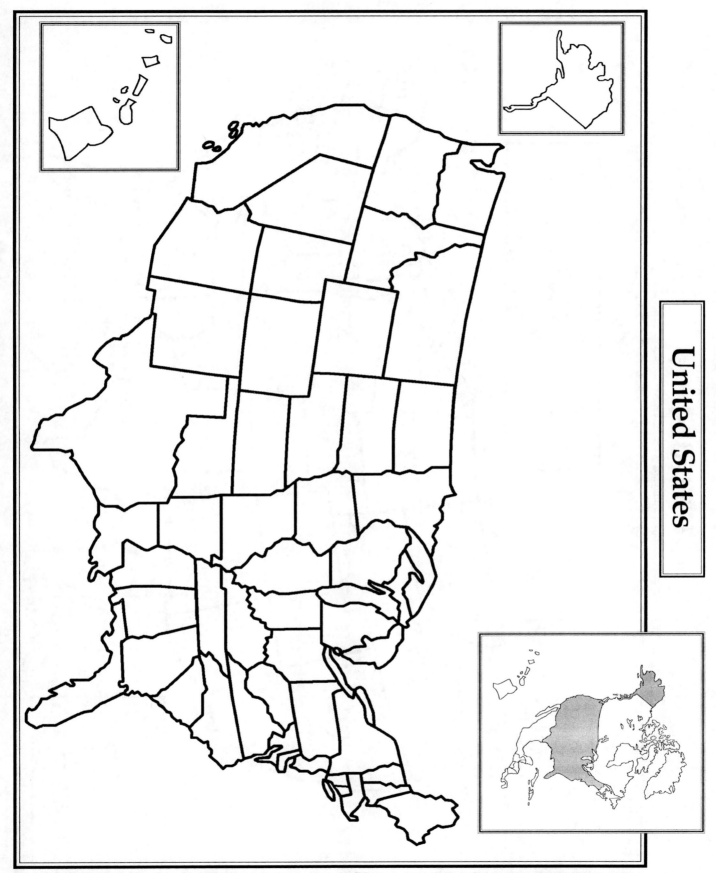

United States

United States

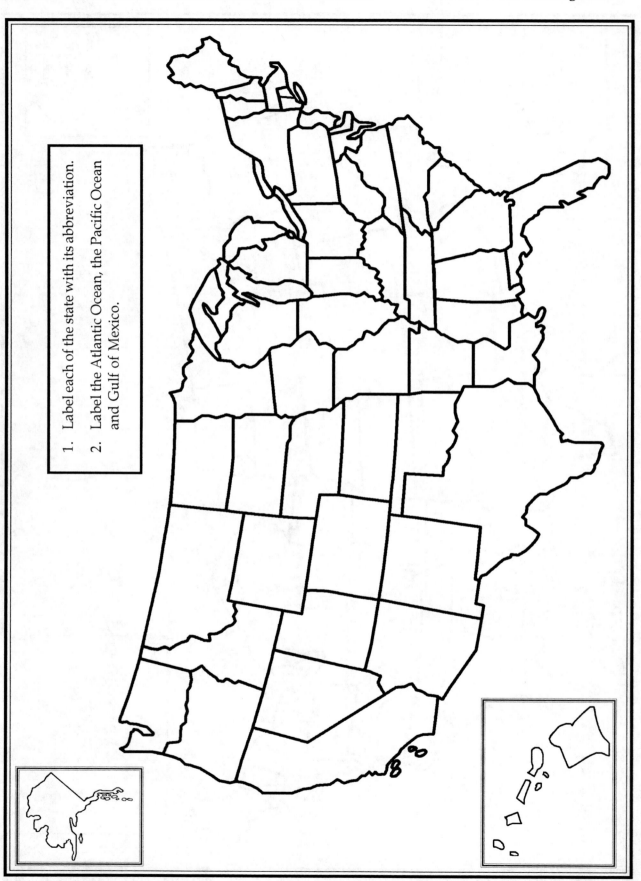

1. Label each of the state with its abbreviation.

2. Label the Atlantic Ocean, the Pacific Ocean and Gulf of Mexico.

Name: _____

Central America

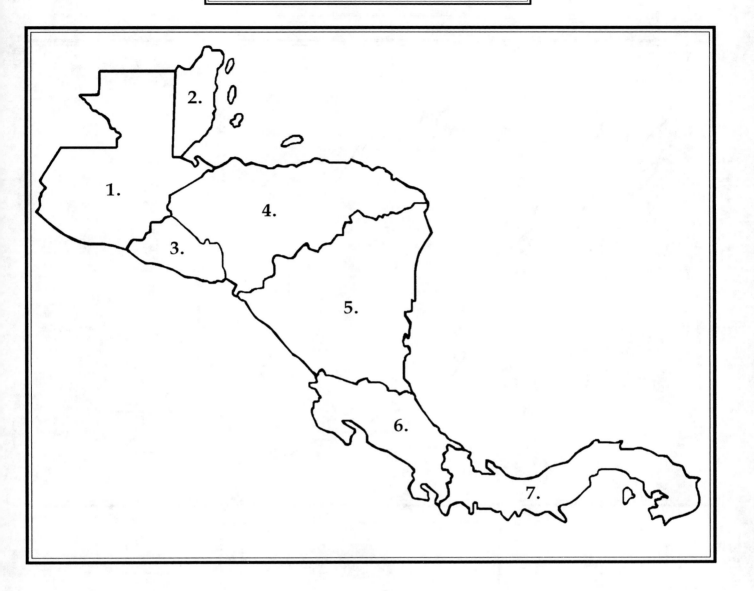

1. _____   5. _____

2. _____   6. _____

3. _____   7. _____

4. _____

Name: _____

Mexico

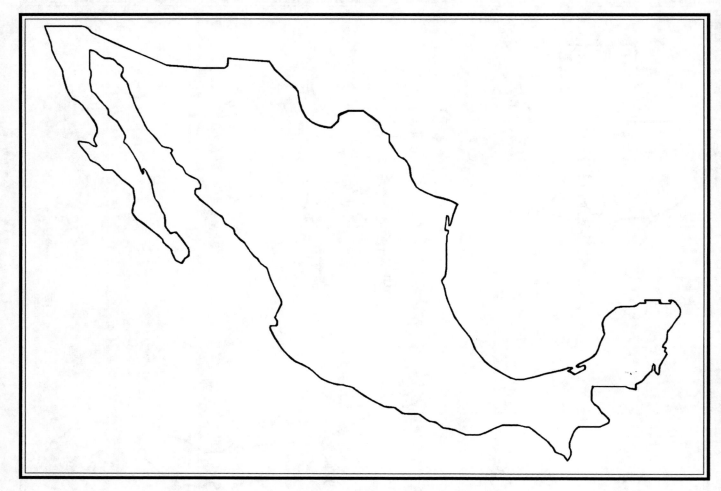

Mexican States

1. _____   12. _____   23. _____

2. _____   13. _____   24. _____

3. _____   14. _____   25. _____

4. _____   15. _____   26. _____

5. _____   16. _____   27. _____

6. _____   17. _____   28. _____

7. _____   18. _____   29. _____

8. _____   19. _____   30. _____

9. _____   20. _____   31. _____

10. _____   21. _____   32. _____

11. _____   22. _____

Caribbean Islands

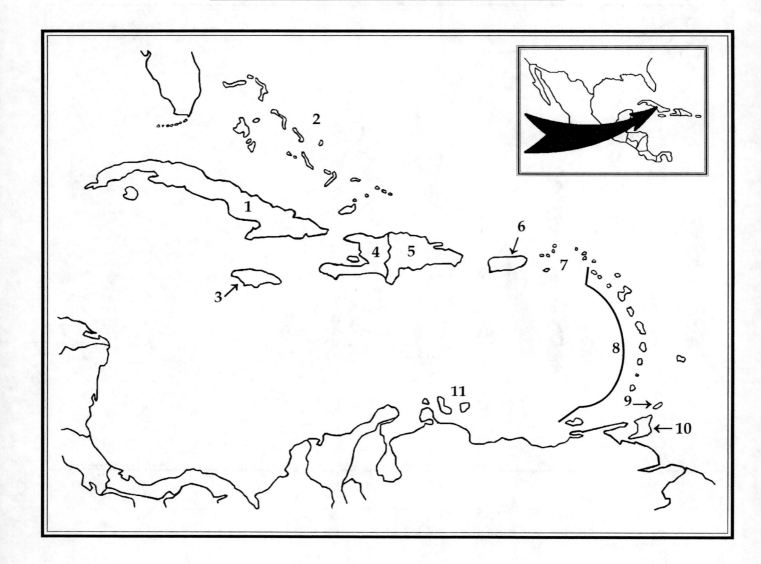

1. _____   7. _____
2. _____   8. _____
3. _____   9. _____
4. _____   10. _____
5. _____   11. _____
6. _____

South America

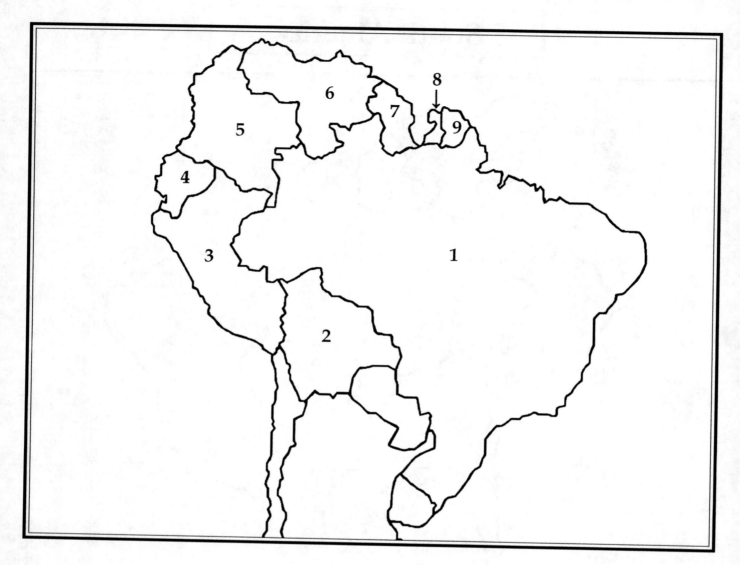

1. _____   8. _____

2. _____   9. _____

3. _____

4. _____

5. _____

6. _____

7. _____

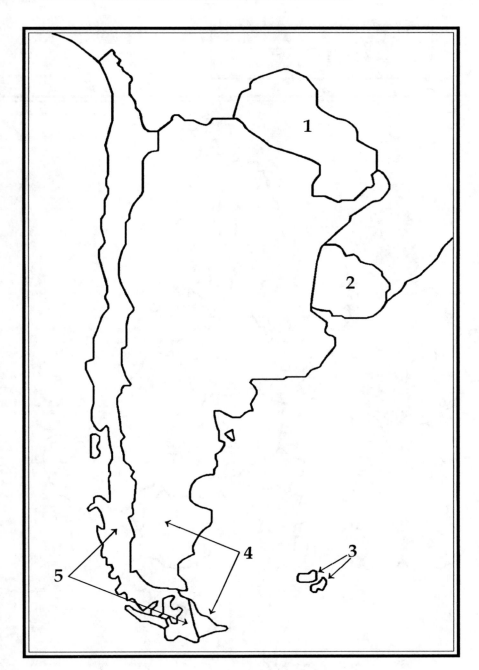

1. _____   4. _____

2. _____   5. _____

3. _____

Name: _____

Europe

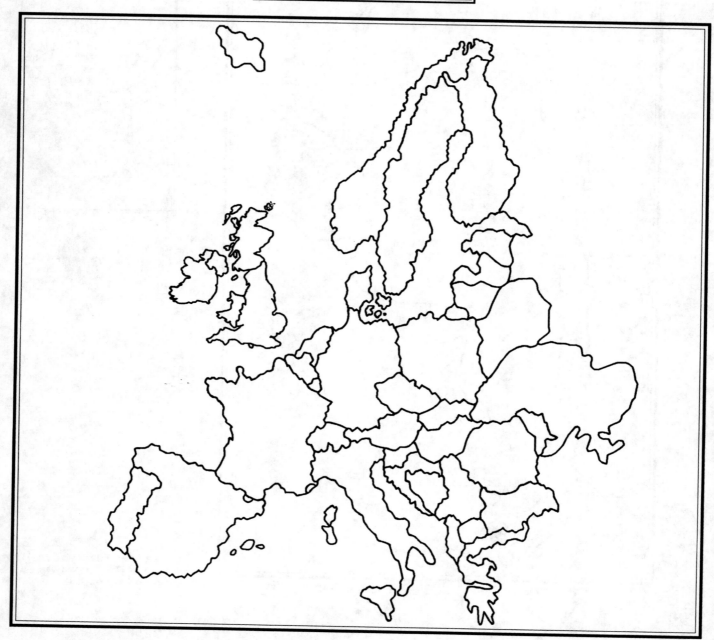

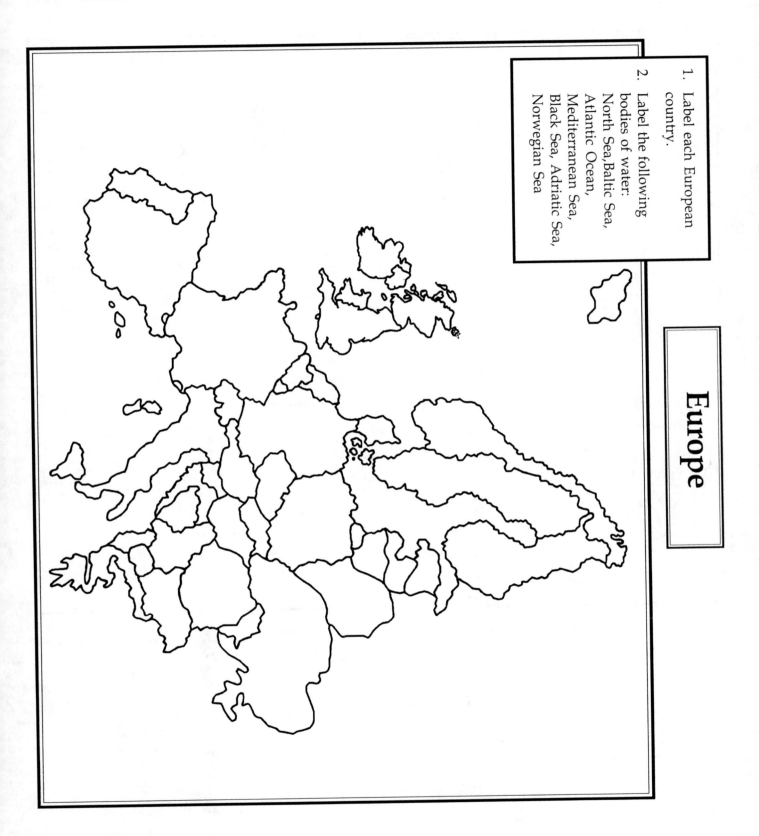

1. Label each European country.

2. Label the following bodies of water:
   North Sea, Baltic Sea, Atlantic Ocean, Mediterranean Sea, Black Sea, Adriatic Sea, Norwegian Sea

Europe

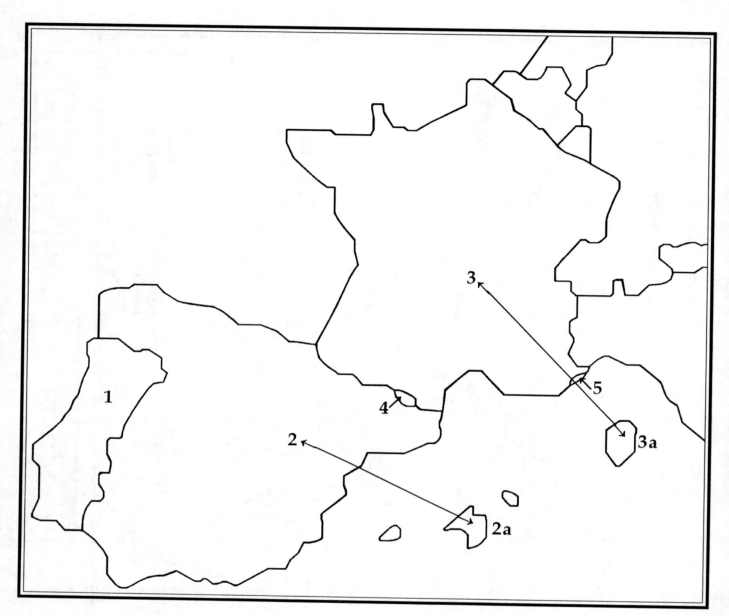

1. _____
2. _____
   a. _____
3. _____
   a. _____
4. _____
5. _____

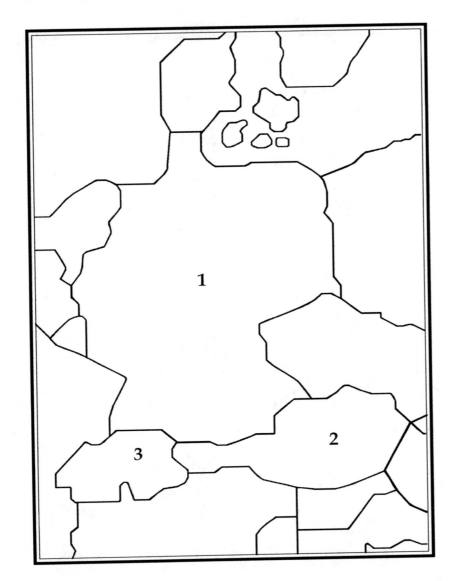

1. _____

2. _____

3. _____

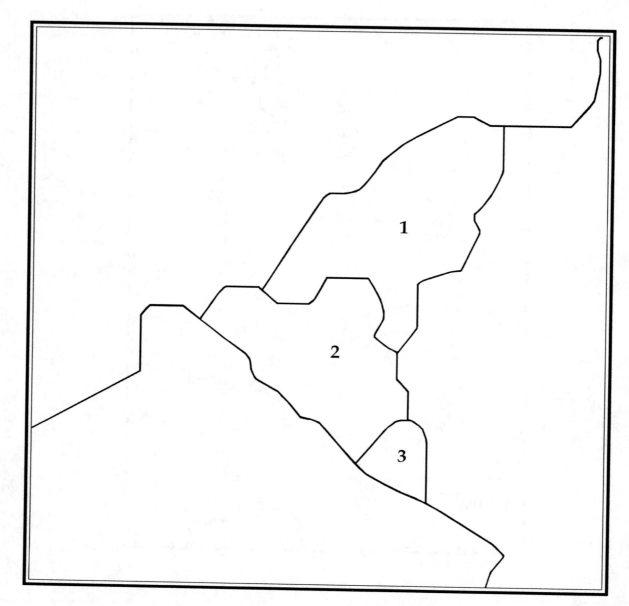

1. _____

2. _____

3. _____

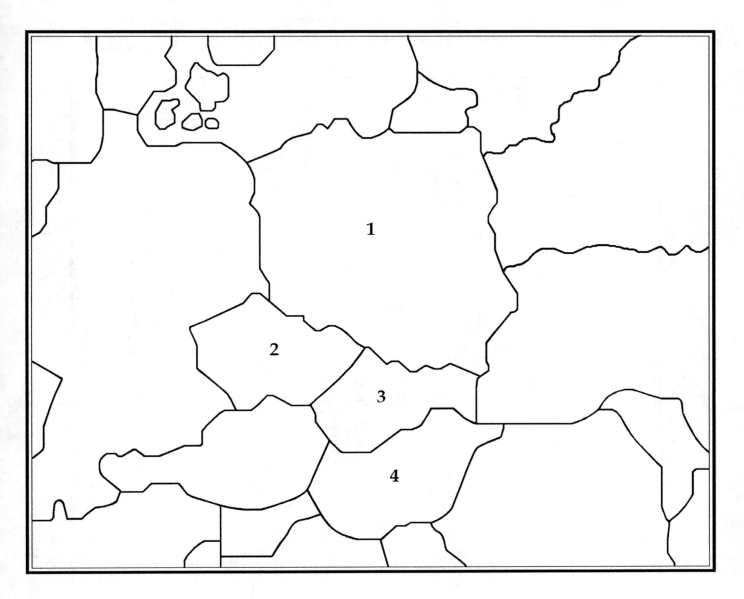

1. _____

2. _____

3. _____

4. _____

Southeastern Europe

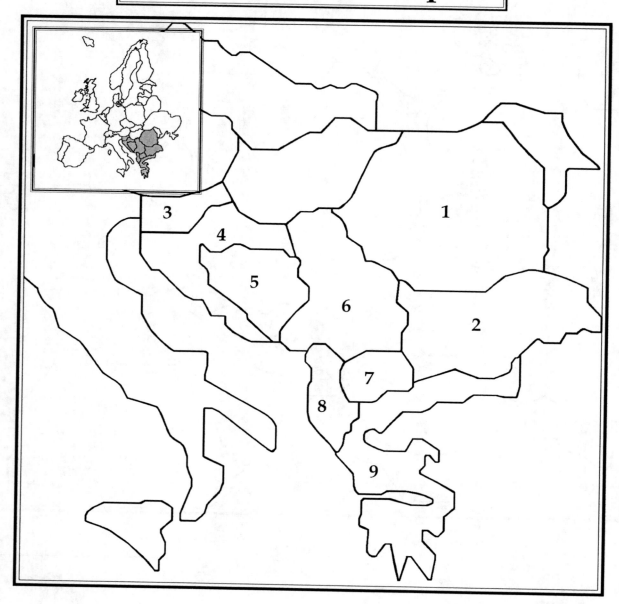

1. _____   6. _____

2. _____   7. _____

3. _____   8. _____

4. _____   9. _____

5. _____

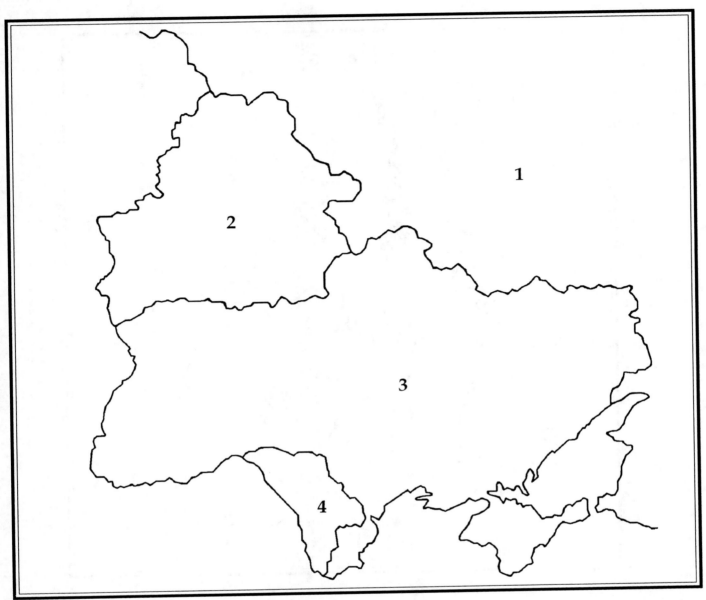

1. _____

2. _____

3. _____

4. _____

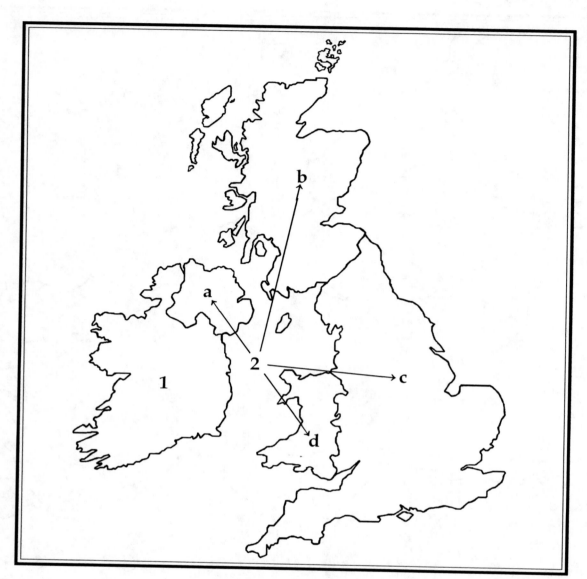

1. _____

2. _____

   a. _____

   b. _____

   c. _____

   d. _____

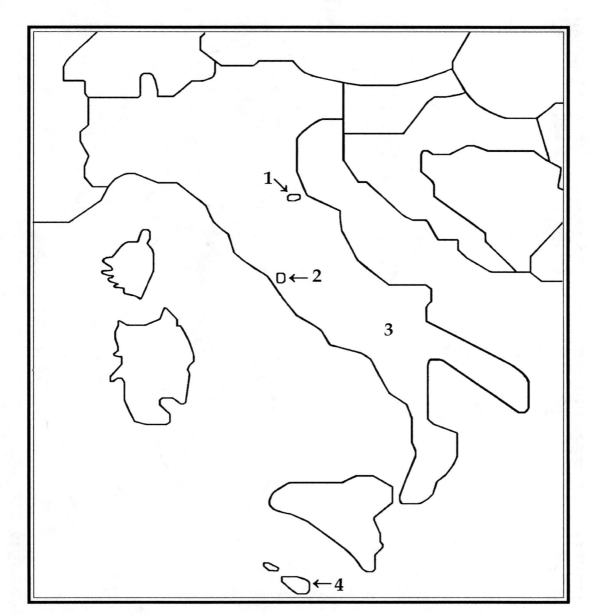

1. _____

2. _____

3. _____

4. _____

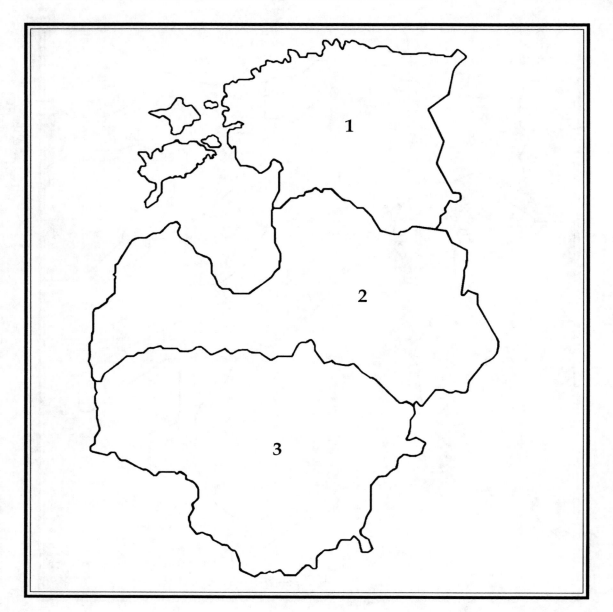

1. _____

2. _____

3. _____

The Balkan States

Slovenia

Croatia

Bosnia and Herzegovina

Romania

Yugoslavia

Bulgaria

Macedonia

Italy

Albania

Turkey

Greece

Crete

Name: _____

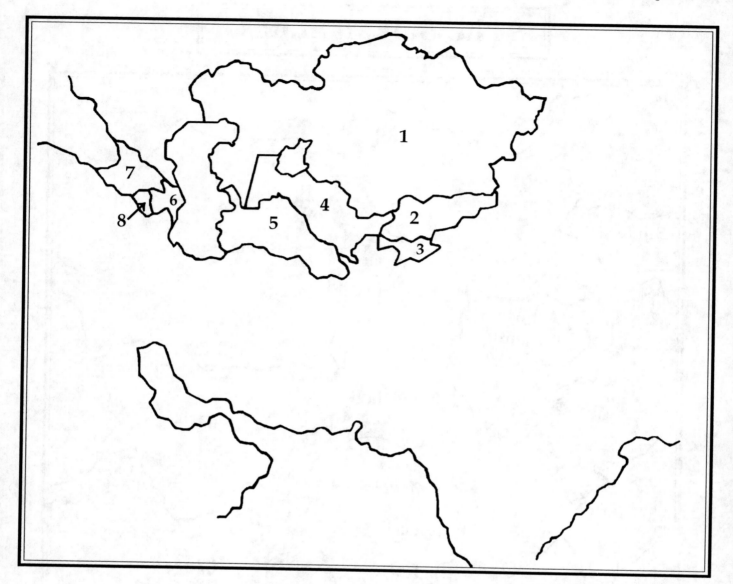

1. _____
2. _____
3. _____
4. _____
5. _____
6. _____
7. _____
8. _____

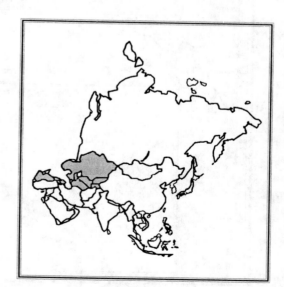

Russia

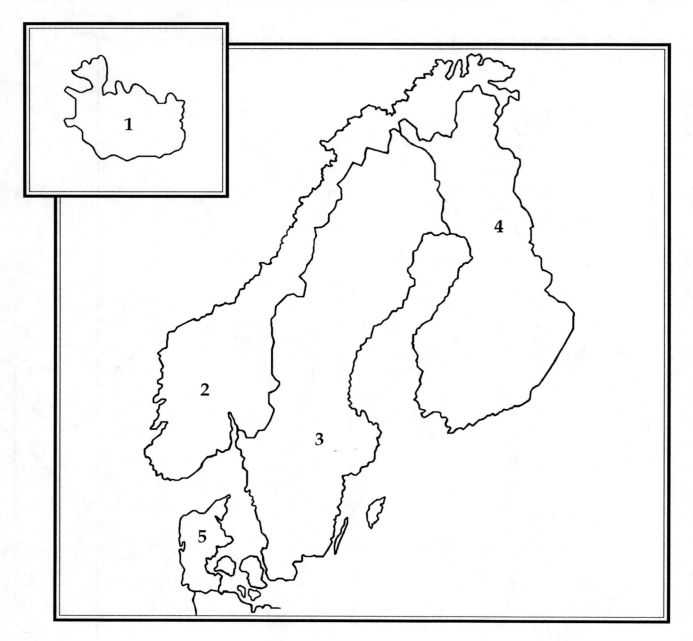

1. _____

2. _____

3. _____

4. _____

5. _____

Africa

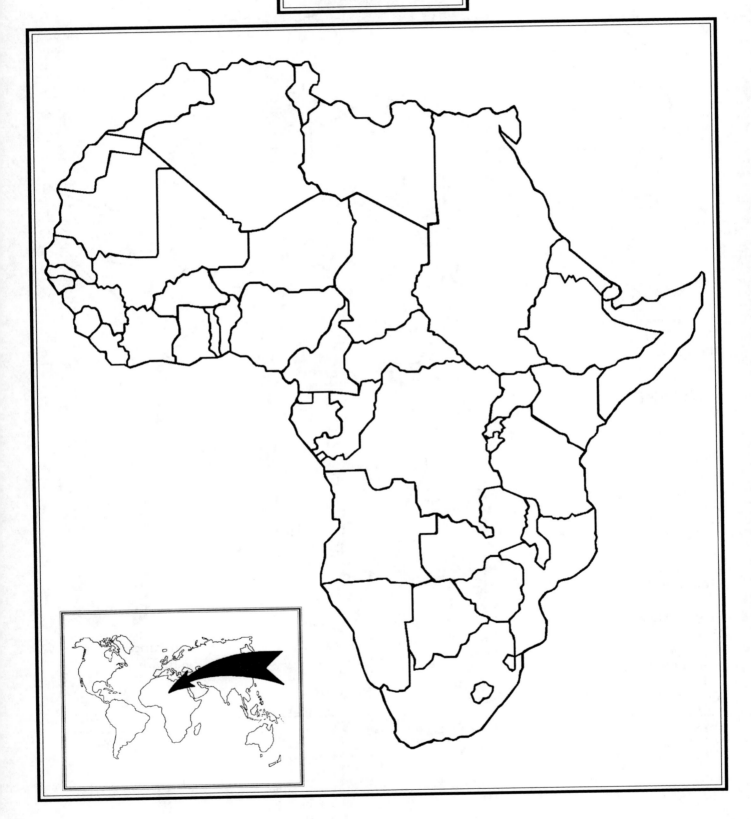

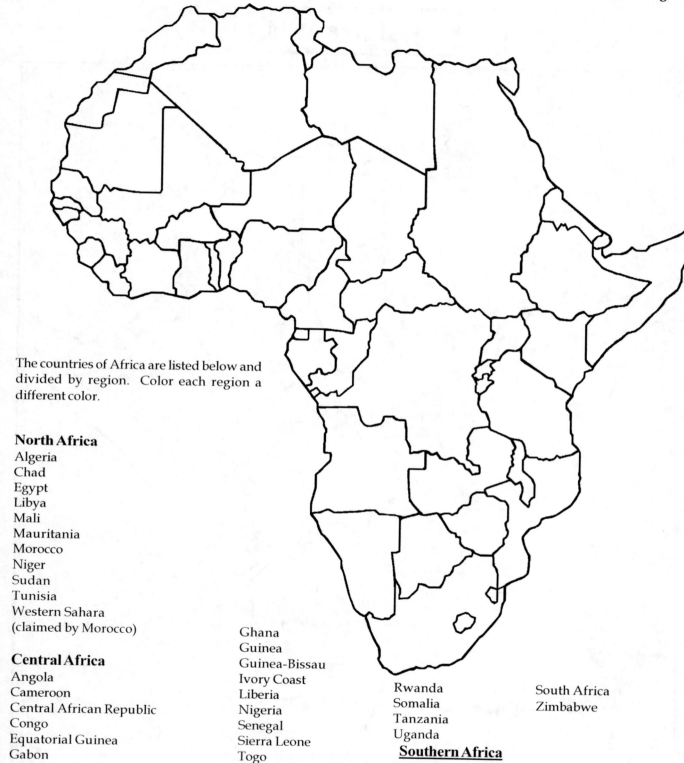

The countries of Africa are listed below and divided by region. Color each region a different color.

North Africa
Algeria
Chad
Egypt
Libya
Mali
Mauritania
Morocco
Niger
Sudan
Tunisia
Western Sahara
(claimed by Morocco)

Central Africa
Angola
Cameroon
Central African Republic
Congo
Equatorial Guinea
Gabon
Zaire
Zambia

<u>**West Africa**</u>
Benin
Burkina Faso
Gambia

Ghana
Guinea
Guinea-Bissau
Ivory Coast
Liberia
Nigeria
Senegal
Sierra Leone
Togo

East Africa
Burundi
Gjibouti
Ethiopia
Tritrea
Kenya

Rwanda
Somalia
Tanzania
Uganda

<u>**Southern Africa**</u>
Botswana
Lesotho
Madagascar
Malawi
Mozambique
Namibia
Swaziland

South Africa
Zimbabwe

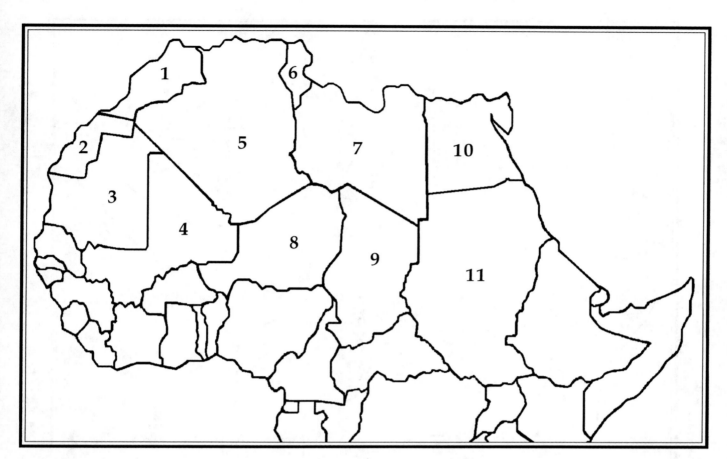

1. _____

2. _____

3. _____

4. _____

5. _____

6. _____

7. _____

8. _____

9. _____

10. _____

11. _____

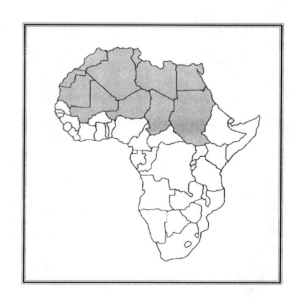

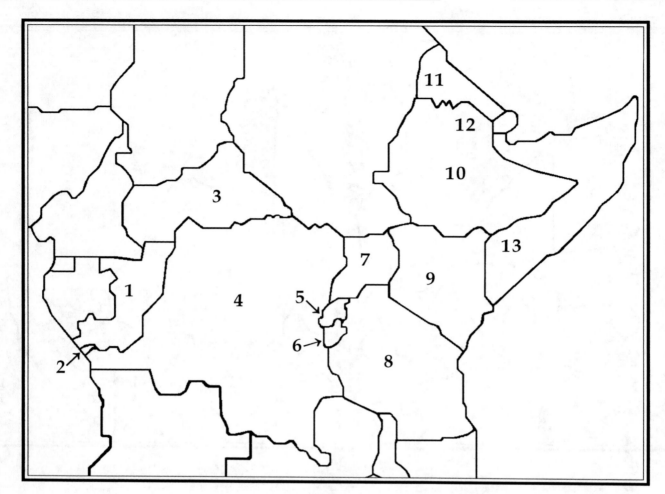

1. _____   10. _____

2. _____   11. _____

3. _____   12. _____

4. _____   13. _____

5. _____

6. _____

7. _____

8. _____

9. _____

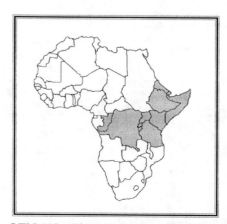

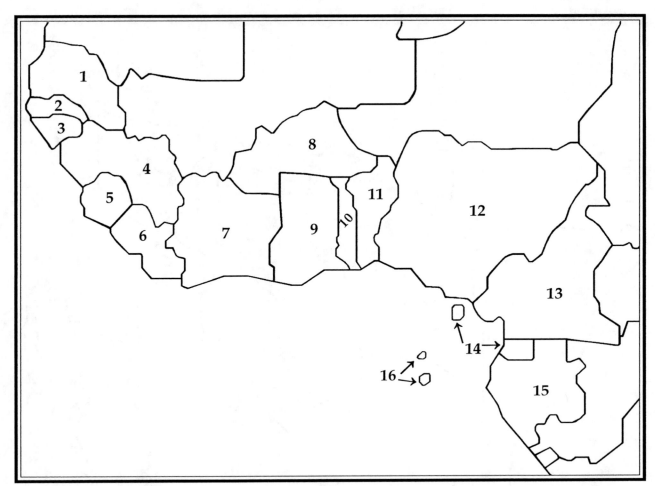

1. _____

2. _____

3. _____

4. _____

5. _____

6. _____

7. _____

8. _____

9. _____

10. _____

11. _____

12. _____

13. _____

14. _____

15. _____

16. _____

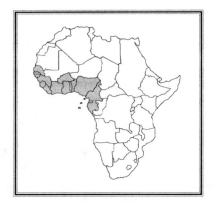

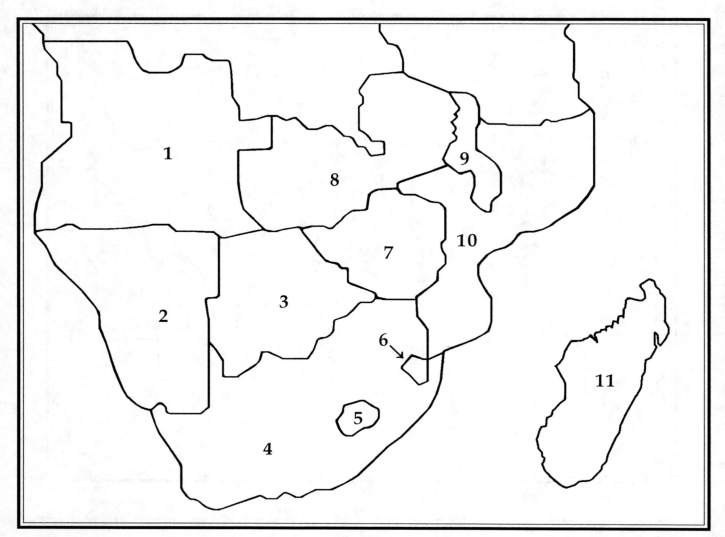

1. _____
2. _____
3. _____
4. _____
5. _____
6. _____
7. _____
8. _____

9. _____
10. _____
11. _____

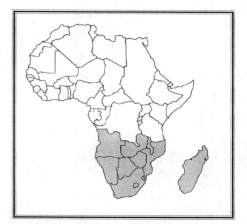

Asia

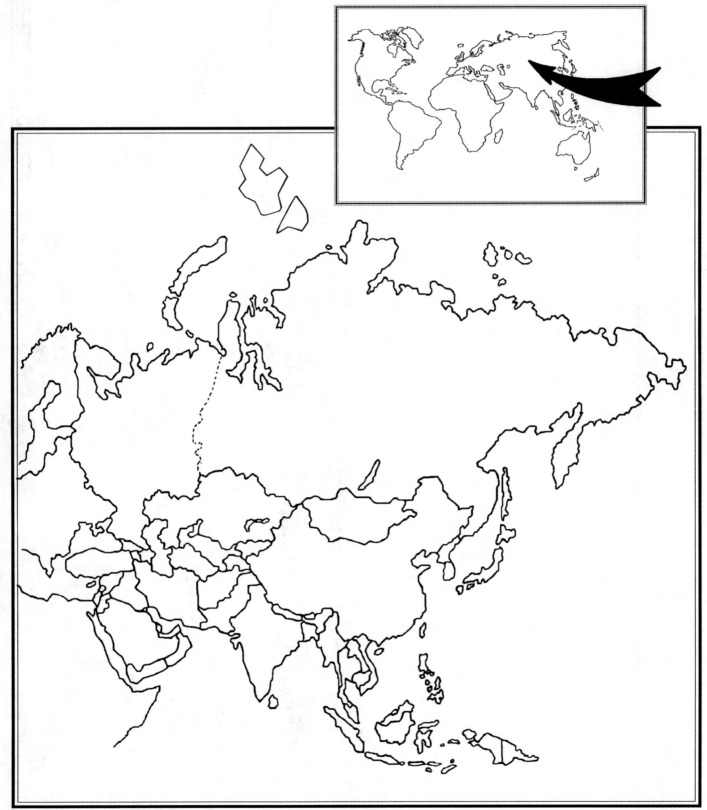

Asia

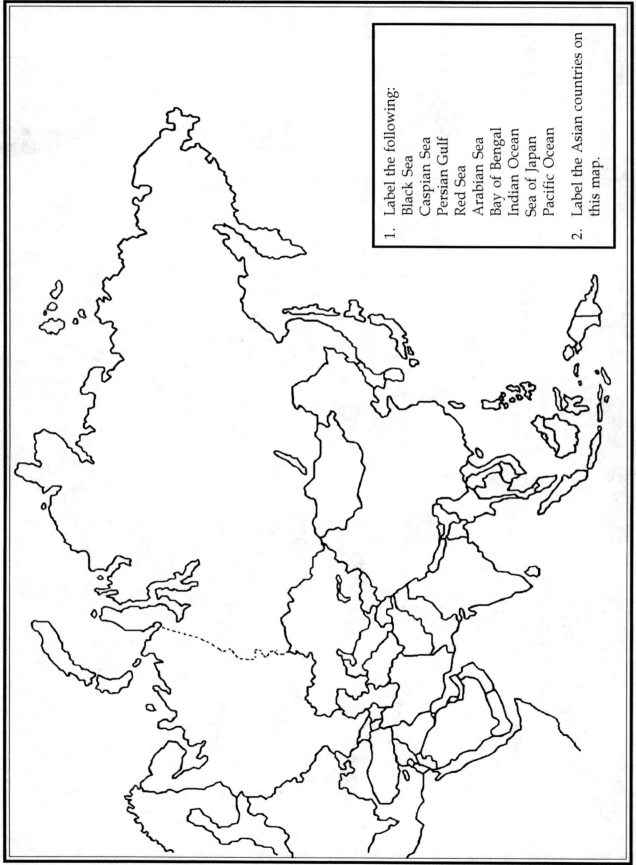

1. Label the following:
   Black Sea
   Caspian Sea
   Persian Gulf
   Red Sea
   Arabian Sea
   Bay of Bengal
   Indian Ocean
   Sea of Japan
   Pacific Ocean

2. Label the Asian countries on this map.

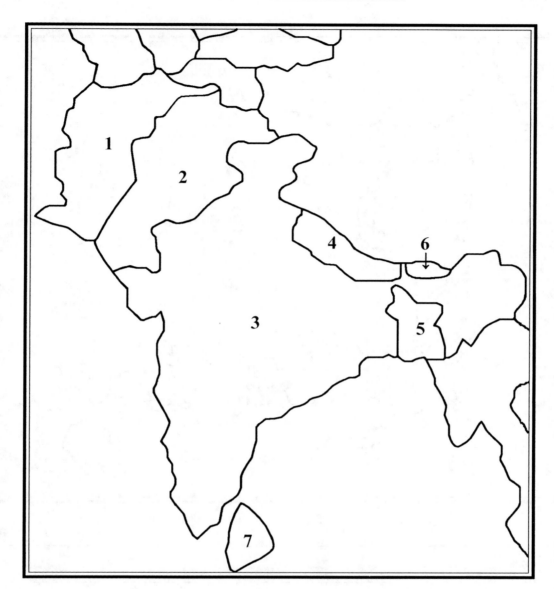

1. _____

2. _____

3. _____

4. _____

5. _____

6. _____

7. _____

8. _____

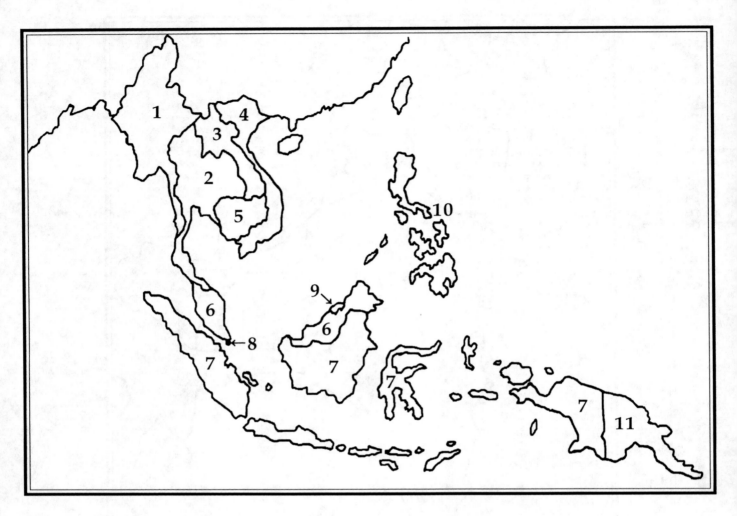

1. _____   10. _____

2. _____   11. _____

3. _____

4. _____

5. _____

6. _____

7. _____

8. _____

9. _____

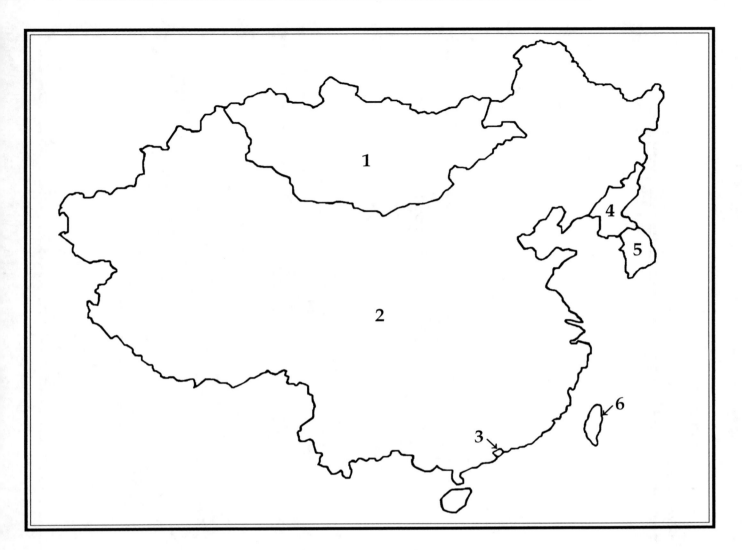

1. _____

2. _____

3. _____

4. _____

5. _____

6. _____

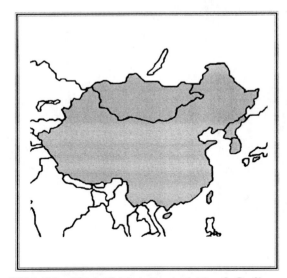

China

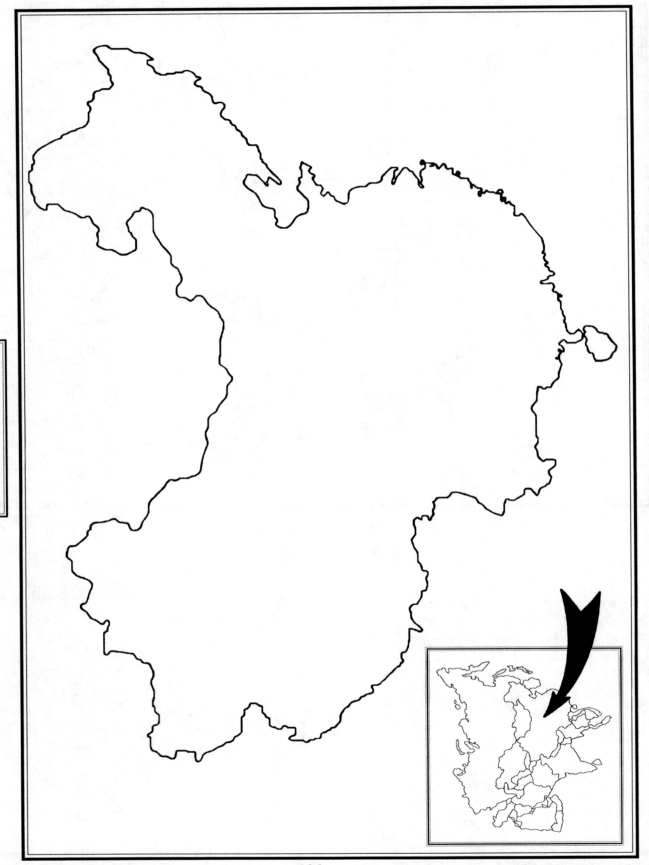

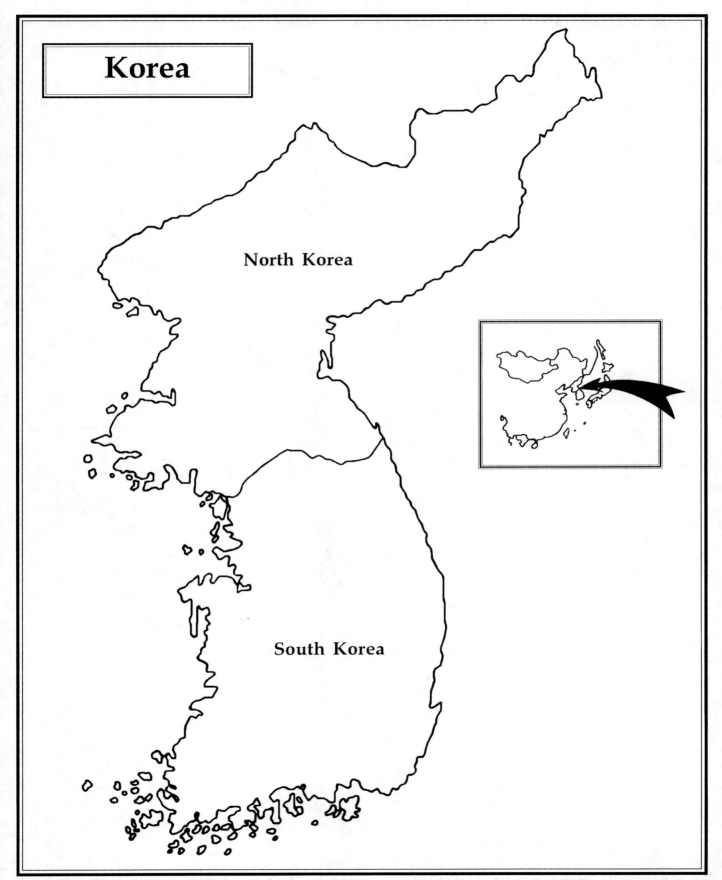

Korea

North Korea

South Korea

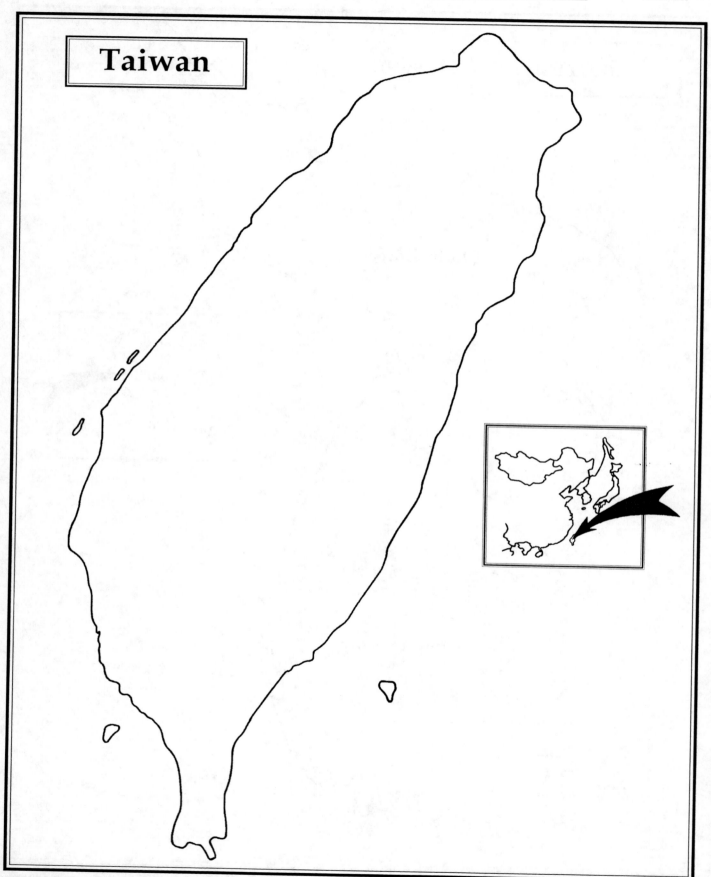

Taiwan

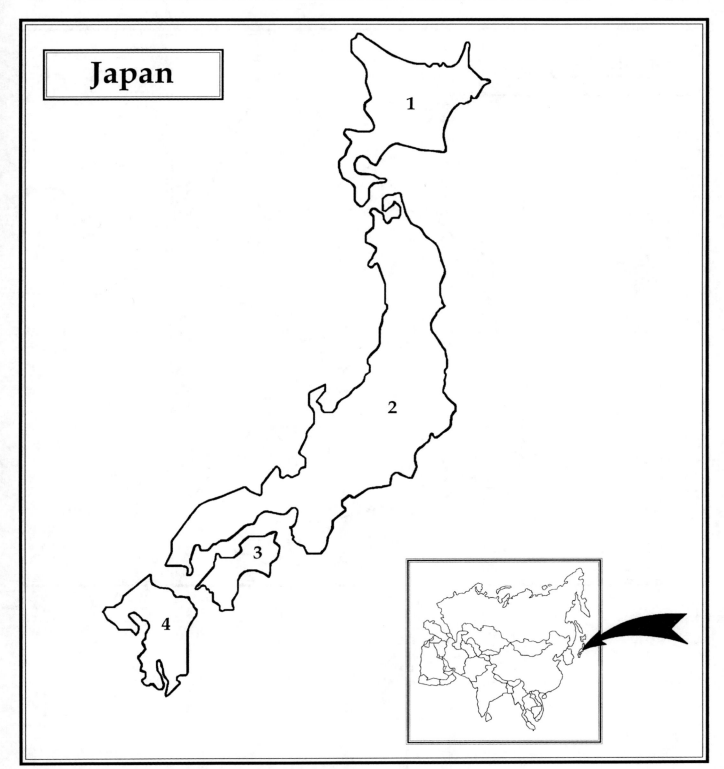

Japan

1. _____   3. _____

2. _____   4. _____

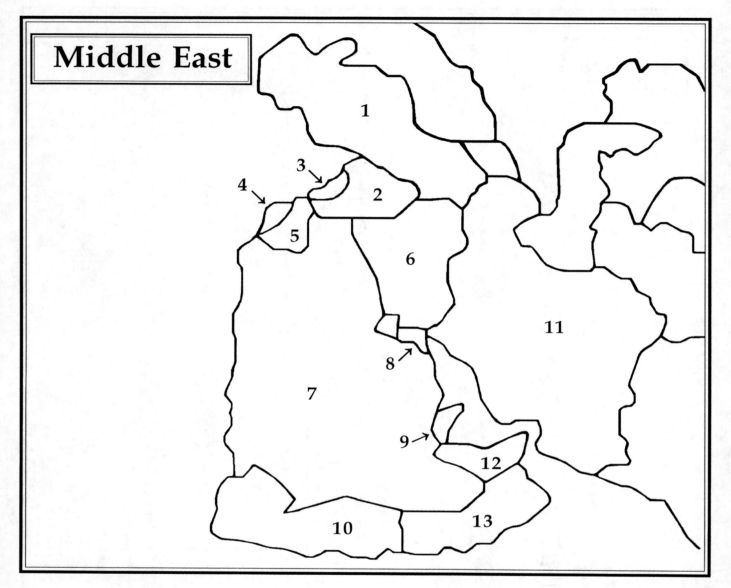

Middle East

1

3

4

2

5

6

7

8

9

11

12

10

13

1. _____

2. _____

3. _____

4. _____

5. _____

6. _____

7. _____

8. _____

9. _____

10. _____

11. _____

12. _____

13. _____

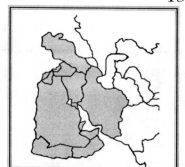

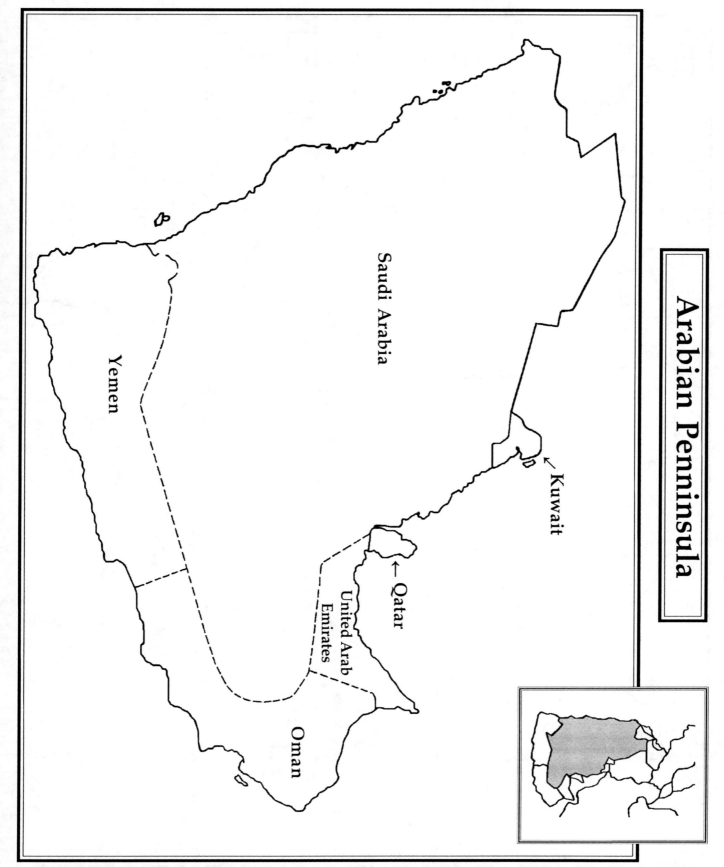

Arabian Penninsula

Saudi Arabia

Yemen

Kuwait

Qatar

United Arab Emirates

Oman

Afghanistan and Pakistan

Afghanistan

Pakistan

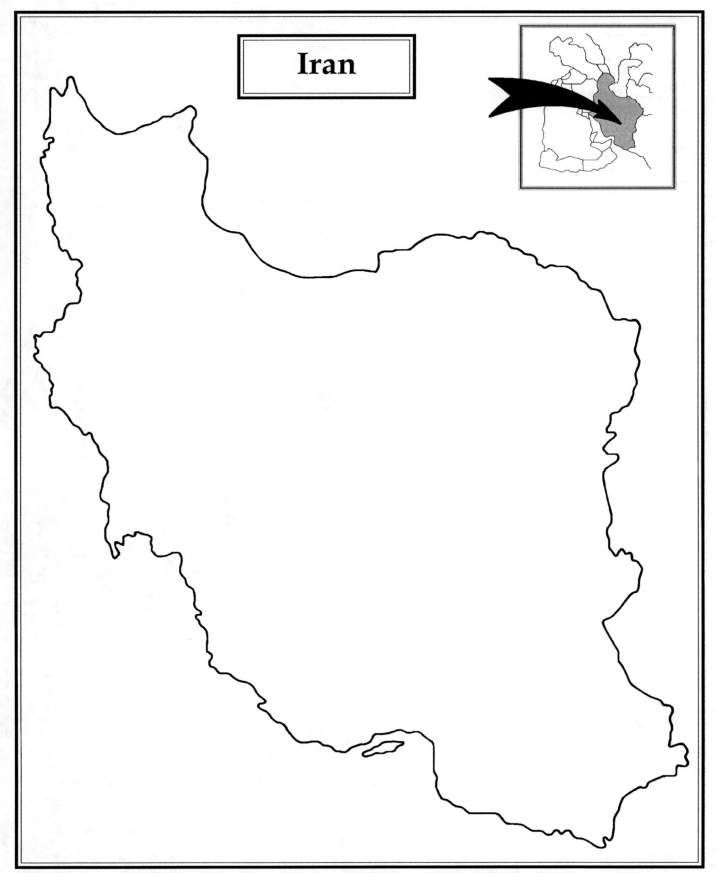

Iran

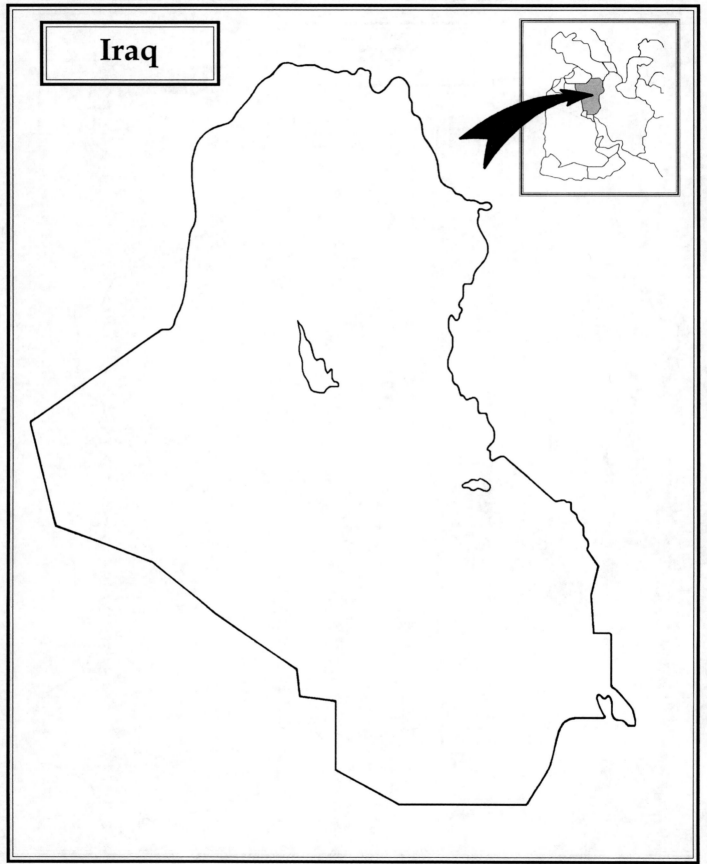

Iraq

Israel

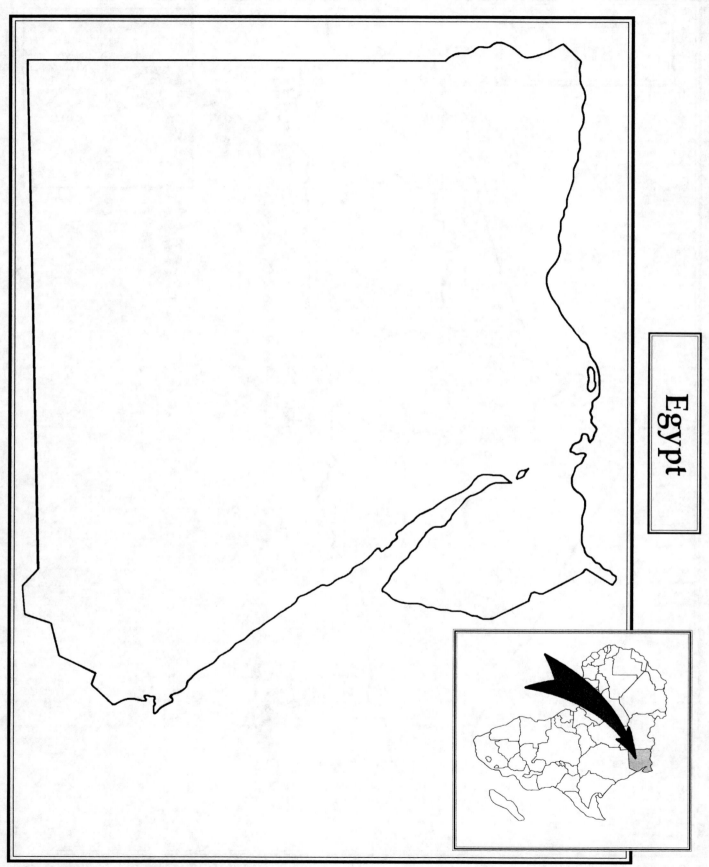

Egypt

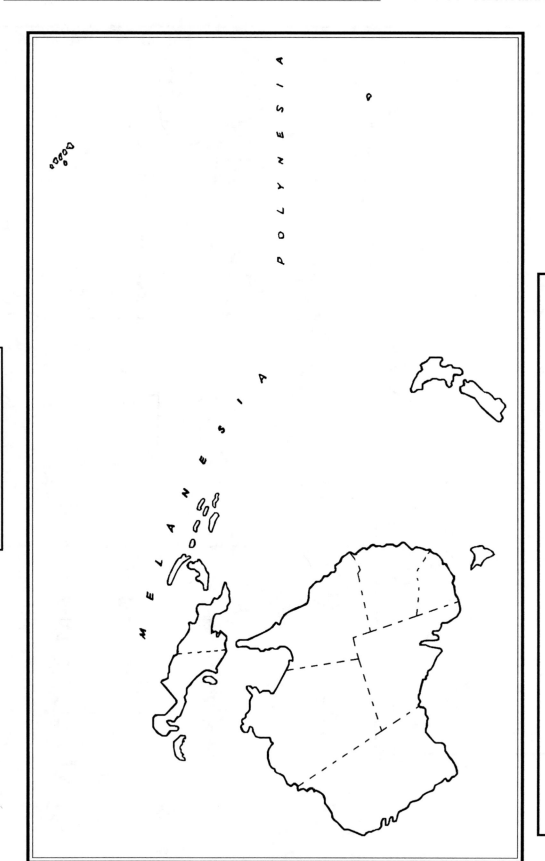

Oceania

1. Label Australia, New Zealand, Papua New Guinea, Melanesia, and Polynesia.

2. Label the two main islands of New Zealand.

3. Label the territories of Australia.

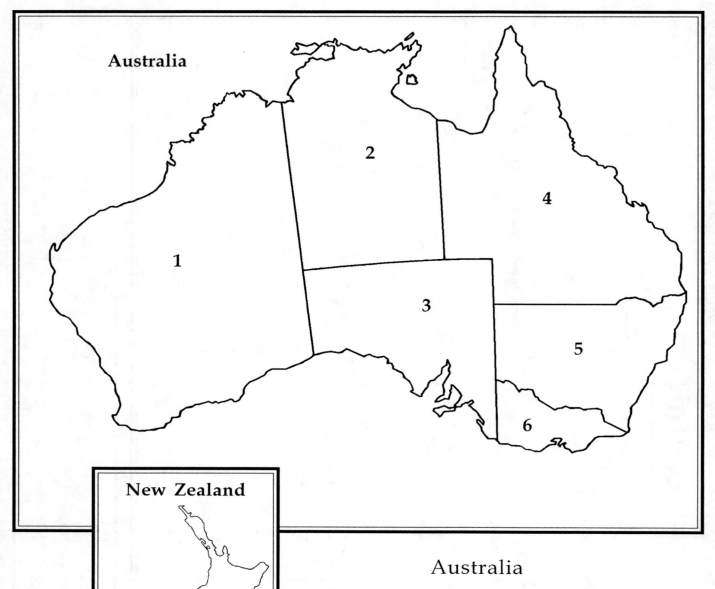

New Zealand

1. _____

2. _____

Australia

1. _____

2. _____

3. _____

4. _____

5. _____

6. _____

7. _____

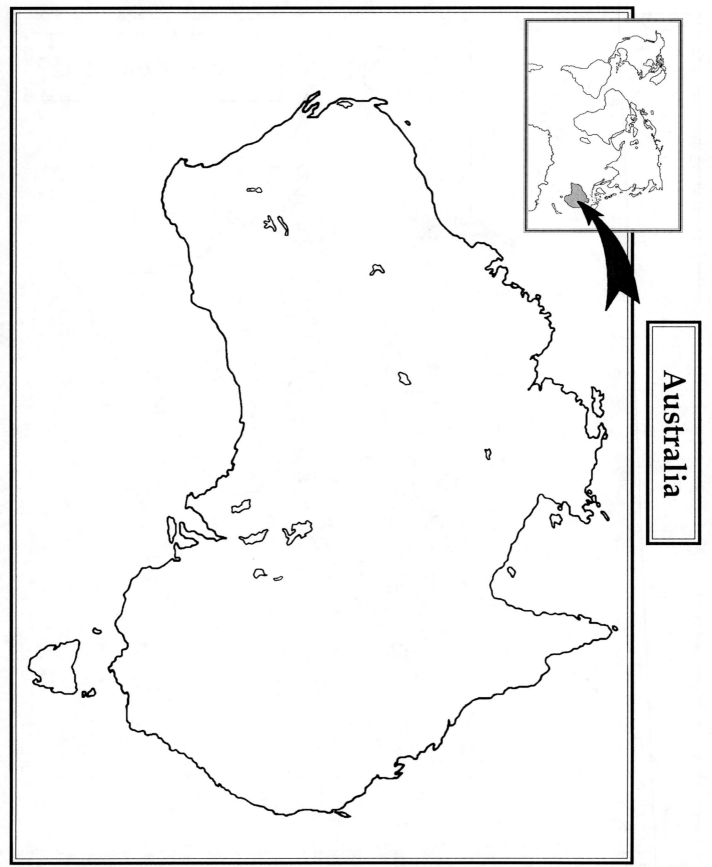

Australia

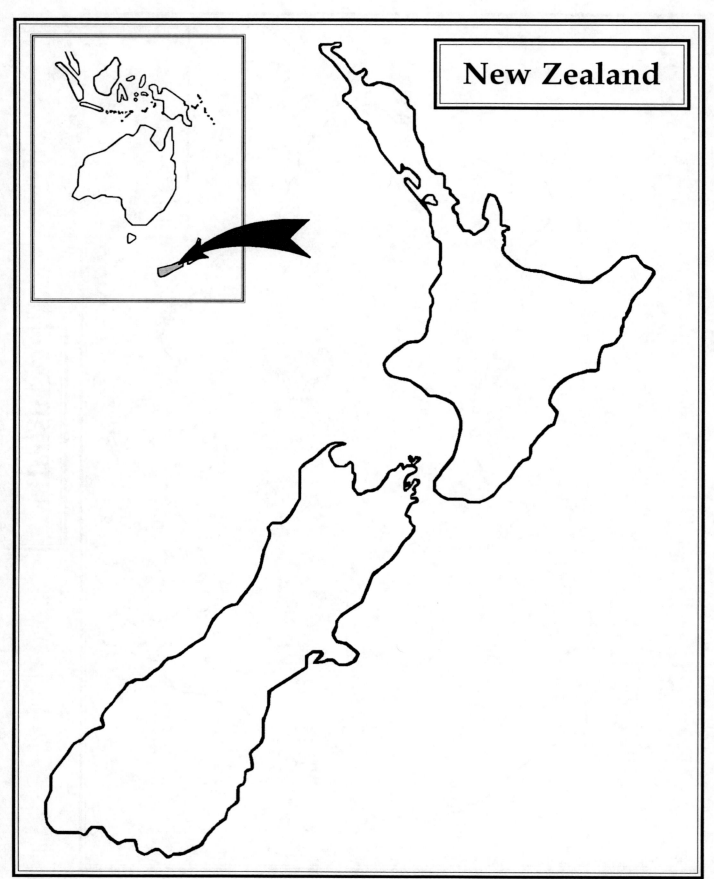

New Zealand

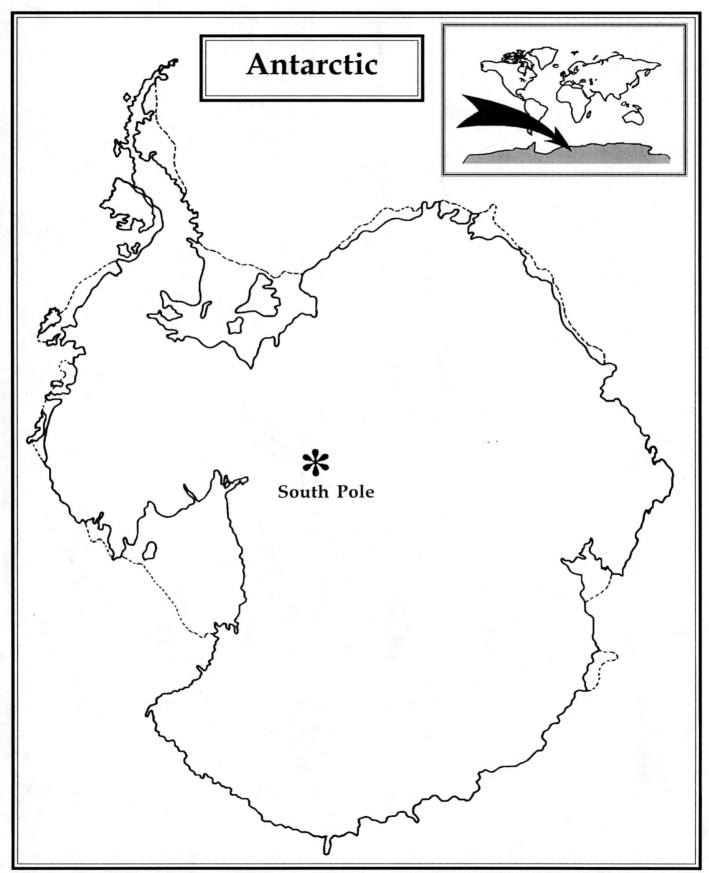

Antarctic

South Pole

121

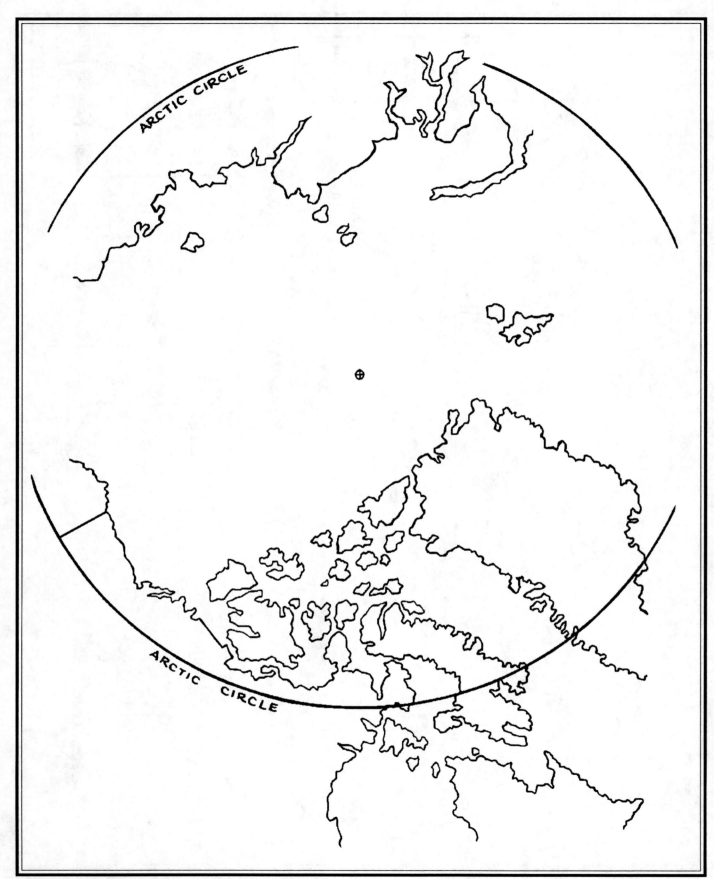

Answer Key
Mapping Skills Activities

What is a Map?: *(page 18)*
Paragraph 1: map, picture, earth, diagram, city, country, continent, world
Paragraph 2: land, water, roads, buildings, trees, flat
   3. Canada   4. west coast   5. North America
   6. Alaska, United States, Alberta

1. Maps are used to find places, measure distances, plan trips and holidays, find the way to places, navigate the ocean and the air, and gain information about a place.
2. Certain maps tell us the population of a country and its location;the climate of a country; transportation routes; where minerals are located; the types of vegetation and location; the types of physical features and their location; where crops are grown; where livestock is raised; where countries are located; the location of oceans, seas, rivers and lakes; areas that receive different amounts of rainfall; where animals live; etc.
3. Cartography is the study and the making of maps.
4. A cartographer is a person who makes maps.

Kinds of Maps: *(page 19)*
1. a) general reference maps; mobility maps; thematic maps
2. a) political boundaries or borders
     b) geographic features   c) bodies of water
     d) cities and towns

     a) maps of provinces and states
     b) maps of countries   c) maps of continents
     d) maps of the world
3. They are usually found in atlases.
4. A political map is one that emphasizes the boundaries of countries, provinces, states and counties.
5. A physical or relief map emphasizes the location of physical features found on the earth's surface such as mountains, valleys, rivers and lakes.

Mobility Maps: *(page 20)*
1. A mobility map is one that helps people find their way from one place to another.
2. They are used for travel on land, on water, and in the air.
3. A chart is a type of map that shows the ocean depths and dangerous underwater rocks. Star charts show the positions of the stars in the sky.
4. Pilots and ship captains use charts to navigate the air and oceans by plane and ship.
5. A road map is the most common mobility map.
6. • different types of roads and highways
   • the location of cities and towns
   • the location of state or provincial parks
   • the location of lakes and rivers
7. street maps, city maps, transit maps, nautical charts, aeronautical charts, county maps, community maps

Thematic Maps: *(page 21)*
1. A thematic map focuses on one particular feature of a country or place.

   natural resources, vegetation areas, population, types of soil, major products, location of minerals, climate, precipitation, temperature, physical features

Inventory Maps: *(page 21)*
1. An inventory map is similar to a thematic map but is more precise. It concentrates on a specific feature. A map that shows every building in a city or community is an inventory map.

Directional Indicators - Part A: *(page 22)*
compass, direction, round, glass-covered, needle, north, north, east, south, west, cardinal, points, intermediate, northeast, southeast, southwest, northwest
   a) northeast, north, east   b) southeast
   c) northwest   d) southwest

Directional Indicators - Part B: *(page 23)*
map, compass rose, cardinal, north, east, south, west, north, south, east, west
   1. north   2. east   3. southwest
   4. northwest   5. southeast   6. northeast
   7. south   8. west, top, north

Map Symbols: *(page 24)*
symbol, drawings, maps, represents, easily, legend, key, information, opens, legend

Map Symbols Used in Atlases: *(page 25)*
   1. international boundary   2. other boundary
   3. capital city of a country   4. other capital
   5. city or town   6. river
   7. seasonal river   8. mountain peak
   9. mountain pass   10. bridge
   11. lake   12. seasonal lake
   13. Dry Lake   14. canal
   15. swamp   16. desert
   17. ruins   18. roads
   19. highway numbers   20. railroad

A Map Tells Distance: *(page 25)*
bar scale, ruler, measuring tape, long
Scale means size. Drawing or making anything to scale means to make a copy which is exactly like the real thing except for size.

scale, drawings, large, centimeter (inch), meter (yard) kilometer (mile)

What is a Globe?: *(page 26)*
globe, earth, roundness, world, stand, spin, rotates
map, pasted, printed, sphere, terrestrial
triangular, gores, world map, lands, seas, shapes, positions

How are Globes Used: *(page 27)*
1. • in the study of geography
   • to help plan air and sea routes
   • in establishing satellite communications
2. It gives a true picture of the earth as a whole. A globe represents all parts of the earth's surface true to scale. Distances, areas and directions are not distorted as they are on flat maps.

Hemispheres: *(page 27)*
1. A hemisphere is one-half of a sphere. It is a name given to any half of the globe.
2. The globe is divided into four main hemispheres.
3. the northern and southern hemispheres, the eastern and western hemispheres, the land and water hemispheres, the daylight and darkness hemispheres

The Northern and Southern Hemispheres: *(page 27)*
equator, boundary, north, northern, south, southern
   A) northern hemisphere   **B)** southern hemisphere

The Eastern and Western Hemispheres: *(page 28)*
natural, dividing, line, Europe, Asia, Africa, Australia, North America, South America
   A) eastern hemisphere   **B)** western hemisphere

Land and Water Hemispheres: *(page 28)*
half, most, London, England, water, water hemisphere, New Zealand

Daylight and Darkness Hemispheres: *(page 28)*
daylight, darkness, boundary, line, twilight, dusk, dawn, rotates

Lines on the Globe: *(page 28)*
Geographic grids, lines, locate, parallels, latitude, meridians, lines, longitude, east, west, equator, degrees, earth's poles, equator, zero, degrees, 90^0, North, 90^0, South, Degrees, 60, longitude, meridians, Greenwich, prime, meridian, north, south, meet, decreases

Parallels of Latitude: *(page 29)*
   1. Arctic Circle   2. Tropic of Cancer
   3. Equator   4. Tropic of Capricorn
   5. Antarctic Circle

Day and Night: *(page 30)*
solar, earth, Day, sun, Night, dark, away
midnight, two, twelve, midnight, noon, a.m., noon, midnight, p.m.
daylight, tilt, axis, pole, slant, North, South, dark, away, dark, sunlight

The Seasons: *(page 30)*
four, spring, summer, autumn, winter, three, temperature, weather, length of daylight,
warmer, longer, hot, warm,
cooler, shorten, cold, shorter
changing, position, North Pole, northern, most, least, winter, starts, autumn
June 21, solstice, longest, winter, December 21, shortest, spring, March 21, September 21, 22, 12, sunlight, 12, darkness

Basic Mapping Skills Card #1: *(page 31)*
Symbols should be colored as instructed.

Basic Mapping Skills Card #2: *(page 32)*
   1. west   2. east   3. south   4. south
   5. north   6. west, road

Basic Mapping Skills Card #3: *(page 33)*
Streets should be colored as indicated.

Basic Mapping Skills Card#4: *(page 33)*
   1. east   2. south
   3. east, Spirit Town, Gremlin City
   4. south   5. north

Basic Mapping Skills Card #5: *(page 34)*
   1. north   2. Royal, Queen
   3. Royal Avenue   4. Elizabeth Avenue
   5. north, south, east   6. library
   7. Royal Avenue   8. east, west
   9. market, meat shop   10. King, Royal

Basic Mapping Skills Card #6: *(page 35)*
Map must contain all the symbols as directed.

Basic Mapping Skills Card #7: *(page 36)*
   1. bridge   2. mountains   3. lake
   4. boundary line   5. river   6. railroad
   7. highway   8. city

Basic Mapping Skills Card #8: *(page 36)*
The map must contain all the features indicated in the instructions.

Basic Mapping Skills Card #9: *(page 37)*
The map must be completed as indicated in the instructions.

Basic Mapping Skills Card #10: *(page 38)*
The map must be completed as indicated in the instructions.

Basic Mapping Skills Card #11 to 13: *(page 39)*
Answers may vary.

Basic Mapping Skills Card #14: *(page 42)*
13 cm; 65 km
   1. 25   2. 40   3. 55   4. 40
   5. Answers may vary.

Basic Mapping Skills Card #15: *(page 43)*
Answers may vary.

Basic Mapping Skills Card #16: *(page 43)*
Pictures should be accurately done.

Basic Mapping Skills Card #17: *(page 44)*
Directions must be followed accurately.

Basic Mapping Skills Card #18: *(page 44)*
Coloring must be done correctly.

Basic Mapping Skills Card #19: *(page 45)*
Two shapes will be made.

Basic Mapping Skills Card #20: *(page 45)*
Answers may vary.

World Mapping Skills Card #1: *(page 46)*
world, continents
   1. North America   2. South America   3. Europe
   4. Africa   5. Asia   6. Australia
   7. Antarctica, oceans

   a) Pacific Ocean   b) Arctic Ocean
   c) Atlantic Ocean   d) Indian Ocean
   e) Southern Ocean

World Mapping Skills Card #2: *(page 47)*
Canada, North America, three, Canada, United States, Mexico, Atlantic Ocean, Pacific Ocean, countries should be colored as indicated, Western Hemisphere

World Mapping Skills Card #3: *(page 48)*
   1. North America   2. Atlantic Ocean
   3. Arctic Ocean   4. Pacific Ocean
   5. Greenland   6. Canada
   7. Canada, United States   8. Mexico
   9. salt water   10. Canada

World Mapping Skills Card #4: *(page 49)*
political, borders, boundaries, provinces, territories, states, countries
   1. Prince Edward Island - Charlottetown, Newfoundland and Labrador - St. John's, Nova Scotia - Halifax, New Brunswick - Fredericton, Québec - Québec City, Ontario - Toronto, Manitoba - Winnipeg, Saskatchewan - Regina, Alberta - Edmonton, British Columbia - Victoria, Yukon - Whitehorse, Northwest Territories - Yellowknife, Nunavut - Iqaluit

2. Prince Edward Island, Newfoundland and Labrador, Nova Scotia, Nunavut, Northwest Territories
3. Arctic Ocean, Pacific Ocean, Atlantic Ocean
4. Nunavut
5. the United States
6. Ottawa, Ontario
7. Prince Edward Island
8. Newfoundland and Labrador
9. Saskatchewan, Alberta
10. Alaska
11. Victoria, British Columbia
12. Manitoba, Saskatchewan, Alberta
13. Nova Scotia, Newfoundland, New Brunswick, Prince Edward Island

World Mapping Skills Card #5: *(page 51)*
1. North America
2. Canada, Mexico
3. 50
4. Washington, Oregon, California, Alaska
5. Texas, Louisiana, Mississippi, Alabama, Florida
6. Alaska, Washington, Idaho, Montana, North Dakota, Minnesota, Michigan, New York, Vermont, New Hampshire, Maine
7. Arkansas River, Missouri River, Ohio River
8. Rio Grande
9. Alaska, Hawaii
10. Hawaii
11. Alaska
12. Wisconsin and Michigan
13. Washington
14. Florida
15. Hawaii
16. Answers may vary.

World Mapping Skills Card #6: *(page 53)*
Answers may vary.

World Mapping Skills Card #7: *(page 54)*
1, 2 and 3. Answers may vary.
4. Pacific Ocean, Atlantic Ocean, Indian Ocean
5. True
6. False
7. Tropic of Cancer, Tropic of Capricorn
8. Names printed on map
9. North
10. South America, Africa, Australia
11. south
12. North America, Asia, Europe, Africa

World Mapping Skills Card #8: *(page 56)*
1, 2. Answers may vary.
3. Canada, United States
4. Africa, Australia, New Zealand
5. south, west
6. north, east

World Mapping Skills Card #9: *(page 57)*
1. a) Greenland b) Russia c) Canada d) United States e) Indian Ocean
f) New Zealand g) South America h) Atlantic Ocean i) Pacific Ocean j) Arctic Ocean
k) Mexico l) Australia
2. Answers will vary.
3. Answers may vary.

World Mapping Skills Card #10: *(page 59)*
1. a) Atlantic Ocean b) United States c) Russia d) Russia e) Indian Ocean
f) Canada
2. Allow some variance in coordinates that students give.
a) 20^0S, 140^0E b) 30^0N, 100^0E c) 20^0N, 100^0W d) 40^0N, 0^0 e) 70^0N, 20^0W
f) 40^0S, 180^0E (approx.)

Mapping Word Study Card #1: *(page 61)*

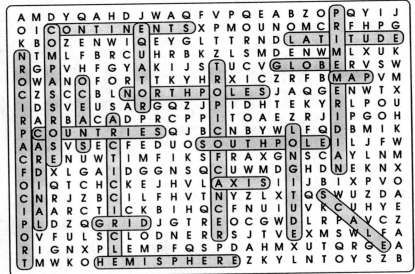

Mapping Word Study Card #2: *(page 62)*

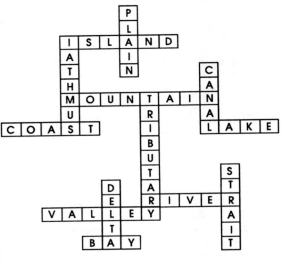

Outline Maps of the World

The World: *(page 66)*
1. Asia   2. Europe   3. Africa   4. Indian Ocean   5. Australia   6. Antarctica
7. Pacific Ocean   8. South America   9. North America   10. Arctic Ocean   11. Atlantic Ocean

North America Countries, Regions & Surrounding Water: *(page 68)*
1.   1. Canada   2. United States   3. Central America   4. Mexico
2.   A) Arctic Ocean   B) Pacific Ocean   C) Gulf of California   D) Gulf of Mexico   E) Atlantic Ocean   F) Panama Canal
3.   Greenland

Canada: *(page 70)*
1.   Provinces:
     1. British Columbia   2. Alberta   3. Saskatchewan   4. Manitoba   5. Ontario   6. Quebec
     7. Newfoundland and Labrador   8. Nova Scotia   9. New Brunswick   10. Prince Edward Island
     11. Nunavut   12. North West Territories   13. Yukon
2.   A) Pacific Ocean   B) Hudson Bay   C) Beaufort Sea   D) Baffin Bay   E) Atlantic Ocean

United States: *(page 72)*
Map of abbreviations

Central America: *(page 73)*
1. Guatemala   2. Belize   3. El Salvador   4. Honduras   5. Nicaragua   6. Costa Rica   7. Panama

Mexican States: *(page 75)*
1. Baja California Norte   2. Baja California Sur   3. Sonora   4. Sinaloa   5. Chihuahua
6. Durango   7. Nayarit   8. Jalisco   9. Zacatecas   10. Coahuila
11. Nuevo Leon   12. Tamaulipas   13. San Luis Potosi   14. Aguascalientes   15. Guanajuato
16. Michoaca   17. Colima   18. Querétaro   19. Hidalgo   20. Veracruz
21. Tiaxcala   22. Puebla   23. Morelos   24. Distrito Federal   25. México
26. Guerrero   27. Oaxaca   28. Chiapas   29. Tabasco   30. Campeche
31. Quintanan Roo   32. Yucatan

Caribbean Islands: *(page 76)*
1. Cuba   2. Bahamas   3. Jamaica   4. Haiti   5. Dominican Republic   6. Puerto Rico
7. Virgin Islands   8. Lesser Antilles   9. Trinidad   10. Tobago   11. Netherlands Antilles

Northern South American Countries: *(page 78)*
1. Brazil   2. Bolivia   3. Peru   4. Ecuador   5. Colombia   6. Venezuela   7. Guyana
8. Suriname   9. French Guiana

Southern South American Countries: *(page 79)*
1. Paraguay   2. Uruguay   3. Falkland Islands (Malvinas)   4. Argentina   5. Chile

Europe: *(page 81)*
1.   1. Belarus   2. Poland   3. Czech Republic
     4. Austria   5. Spain   6. Portugal
     7. Great Britain (England, Scotland, Wales)   8. Ireland
     9. Sweden   10. Lithuania   11. Germany
     12. Iceland   13. Netherlands   14. France
     15. Hungary   16. Italy   17. Norway
     18. Yugoslavia   19. Moldova   20. Denmark
     21. Russia (part)   22. Finland   23. Belgium
     24. Macedonia   25. Slovakia   26. Ukraine

27. Bulgaria   28. Croatia   29. Estonia   30. Romania   31. Latvia
32. Bosnia and Herzegovina   33. Greece   34. Slovenia   35. Albania
36. Switzerland   37. Luxembourg   38. Monaco   39. Andorra
2. **A)** North Sea   **B)** Baltic Sea   **C)** Atlantic Ocean   **D)** Mediter. Sea   **E)** Adriatic Sea
F) Norwegian Sea

Southwestern European Countries: *(page 82)*
1. Portugal   2. Spain   3. France   4. Andorra   5. Monaco

Central European Countries: *(page 83)*
1. Germany   2. Austria   3. Switzerland

Northwestern European Countries: *(page 84)*
1. Netherlands   2. Belgium   3. Luxembourg

Eastern European Countries: *(page 85)*
1. Poland   2. Czech Republic   3. Slovak Republic (Slovakia)   4. Hungary

Southeastern European Countries: *(page 86)*
1. Romania   2. Bulgaria   3. Slovenia   4. Croatia   5. Bosnia and Herzegovina
6. Yugoslavia   7. Macedonia   8. Albania   9. Greece

Northeastern European Countries: *(page 87)*
1. Russia (in Europe)   2. Belarus   3. Ukraine   4. Moldova

United Kingdom & Ireland: *(page 88)*
1. Ireland   2. United Kingdom   **a)** Northern Ireland   **b)** Scotland   **c)** England   **d)** Wales

Italy: *(page 89)*
1. San Marino   2. Vatican City   3. Italy   4. Malta

The Baltic States: *(page 90)*
1. Estonia   2. Latvia   3. Lithuania

Former Soviet Republics: *(page 92)*
1. Kazakhstan   2. Kyrgyzstan   3. Tajikistan   4. Uzbekistan   5. Turkmenistan   6. Azerbaijan
7. Georgia   8. Armenia

Scandinavian Countries: *(page 94)*
1. Iceland   2. Norway   3. Sweden   4. Finland   5. Denmark

African Countries & Regions: *(page 96)*

North Africa
West Africa
Central Africa
East Africa
Southern Africa

Northern African Countries: *(page 97)*
1. Morocco   2. Western Sahara   3. Mauritania   4. Mali   5. Algeria   6. tunisia
7. Libya   8. Niger   9. Chad   10. Egypt   11. Sudan

Central African Countries: *(page 98)*
1. Congo   2. Cabinda   3. Central African Republic   4. Democratic Republic of Congo
5. Rwanda   6. Burundi   7. Uganda   8. Tanzania   9. Kenya
10. Ethiopia   11. Eritrea   12. Djibouti   13. Somalia

Western African Countries: *(page 99)*
1. Senegal   2. Gambia   3. Guinea-Bissau   4. Guinea   5. Sierra Leone   6. Liberia
7. Ivory Coast   8. Burkina Faso   9. Ghana   10. Togo   11. Benin   12. Nigeria
13. Cameroon   14. Equatorial Guinea   15. Gabon   16. Principe and Sao Tome

Southern African Countries: *(page 100)*

1. Angola
2. Namibia
3. Botswana
4. South Africa
5. Lesotho
6. Swaziland
7. Zimbabwe
8. Zambia
9. Malawi
10. Mozambique
11. Somalia

Asian Countries & Bodies of Water: *(page 102)*

1. Turkey
2. Syria
3. Cyprus
4. Lebanon
5. Israel
6. Jordan
7. Iraq
8. Kuwait
9. Bahrain
10. Qatar
11. Saudi Arabia
12. Yemen
13. Oman
14. United Arab Emirates
15. Iran
16. Georgia
17. Armenia
18. Azerbaijan
19. Afghanistan
20. Pakistan
21. Nepal
22. India
23. Bangladesh
24. Sri Lanka
25. Bhutan
26. Maldives
27. Burma
28. Laos
29. Thailand
30. Cambodia
31. Vietnam
32. Malaysia
33. Brunei
34. Indonesia
35. Philippines
36. Singapore
37. China
38. Japan
39. Mongolia
40. North Korea
41. South Korea
42. Kazakhstan
43. Kygyzstan
44. Russia
45. Tajikistan
46. Turkmenistan
47. Uzbekistan
48. Taiwan
49. Black Sea
50. Caspian Sea
51. Persian Gulf
52. Red Sea
53. Arabian Sea
54. Bay of Bengal
55. Indian Ocean
56. Sea of Japan
57. Pacific Ocean

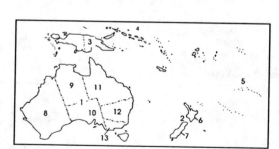

Asian Subcontinent: *(page 103)*

1. Afghanistan
2. Pakistan
3. India
4. Nepal
5. Bangladesh
6. Bhutan
7. Sri Lanka

Southeast Asia: *(page 104)*

1. Burma (Myanmar)
2. Thailand
3. Laos
4. Vietnam
5. Cambodia (Kampuchea)
6. Malaysia
7. Indonesia
8. Singapore
9. Brunei
10. Philippines
11. Papua New Guinea

Far East: *(page 105)*

1. Mongolia
2. China
3. Macau
4. North Korea
5. South Korea
6. Taiwan

Japan: *(page 109)*

1. Hokkaido
2. Honshu
3. Shikoku
4. Kyushu

Countries of the Middle East: *(page 110)*

1. Turkey
2. Syria
3. Lebanon
4. Israel
5. Jordan
6. Iraq
7. Saudi Arabia
8. Kuwait
9. Qatar
10. Yemen
11. Iran
12. United Arab Emirates
13. Oman

Islands of the Central and South Pacific: *(page 117)*

1. Australia
2. New Zealand
3. Papua New Guinea
4. Melanesia
5. Polynesia
6. North Island
7. South Island
8. Western Australia
9. Northern Territory
10. South Australia
11. Queensland
12. New South Wales
13. Victoria

Australia & New Zealand: *(page 118)*

Australia:

1. Western Australia
2. Northern Territory
3. South Australia
4. Queensland
5. New South Wales
6. Victoria
7. Tasmania

New Zealand:

1. North Island
2. South Island

Publication Listing

See Dealer or
www.sslearning.com
For Pricing
1-800-463-6367

Code #	Title and Grade
SSC1-12	A Time of Plenty Gr. 2
SSN1-92	Abel's Island NS 4-6
SSF1-16	Aboriginal Peoples of Canada Gr. 7-8
SSK1-31	Addition & Subtraction Drills Gr. 1-3
SSK1-28	Addition Drills Gr. 1-3
SSY1-04	Addition Gr. 1-3
SSN1-174	Adv. of Huckle Berry Finn NS 7-8
SSB1-63	African Animals Gr 4-6
SSB1-29	All About Bears Gr. 1-2
SSF1-08	All About Boats Gr. 2-3
SSJ1-02	All About Canada Gr. 2
SSB1-54	All About Cattle Gr. 4-6
SSN1-10	All About Colours Gr. P-1
SSB1-93	All About Dinosaurs Gr. 2
SSN1-14	All About Dragons Gr. 3-5
SSB1-07	All About Elephants Gr. 3-4
SSB1-68	All About Fish Gr. 4-6
SSN1-39	All About Giants Gr. 2-3
SSH1-15	All About Jobs Gr. 1-3
SSH1-05	All About Me Gr. 1
SSA1-02	All About Mexico Gr. 4-6
SSR1-28	All About Nouns Gr. 5-7
SSF1-09	All About Planes Gr. 2-3
SSB1-33	All About Plants Gr. 2-3
SSR1-29	All About Pronouns Gr. 5-7
SSB1-12	All About Rabbits Gr. 2-3
SSB1-58	All About Spiders Gr. 4-6
SSA1-03	All About the Desert Gr. 4-6
SSA1-04	All About the Ocean Gr. 5-7
SSZ1-01	All About the Olympics Gr. 2-4
SSB1-49	All About the Sea Gr. 4-6
SSK1-06	All About Time Gr. 4-6
SSF1-07	All About Trains Gr. 2-3
SSH1-18	All About Transportation Gr. 2
SSB1-01	All About Trees Gr. 4-6
SSB1-61	All About Weather Gr. 7-8
SSB1-06	All About Whales Gr. 3-4
SSPC-26	All Kinds of Clocks B/W Pictures
SSB1-110	All Kinds of Structures Gr. 1
SSH1-19	All Kinds of Vehicles Gr. 3
SSF1-01	Amazing Aztecs Gr. 4-6
SSB1-92	Amazing Earthworms Gr. 2-3
SSJ1-50	Amazing Facts in Canadian History Gr. 4-6
SSB1-32	Amazing Insects Gr. 4-6
SSN1-132	Amelia Bedelia–Camping NS 1-3
SSN1-68	Amelia Bedelia NS 1-3
SSN1-155	Amelia Bedelia-Surprise Shower NS 1-3
SSA1-13	America The Beautiful Gr. 4-6
SSN1-57	Amish Adventure NS 7-8
SSF1-02	Ancient China Gr. 4-6
SSF1-18	Ancient Egypt Gr. 4-6
SSF1-21	Ancient Greece Gr. 4-6
SSF1-19	Ancient Rome Gr. 4-6
SSQ1-06	Animal Town – Big Book Pkg 1-3
SSQ1-02	Animals Prepare Winter – Big Book Pkg 1-3
SSN1-150	Animorphs the Invasion NS 4-6
SSN1-53	Anne of Green Gables NS 7-8
SSB1-40	Apple Celebration Gr. 4-6
SSB1-04	Apple Mania Gr. 2-3
SSB1-38	Apples are the Greatest Gr. P-K
SSB1-59	Arctic Animals Gr. 4-6
SSN1-162	Arnold Lobel Author Study Gr. 2-3
SSPC-22	Australia B/W Pictures
SSA1-05	Australia Gr. 5-8
SSM1-03	Autumn in the Woodlot Gr. 2-3
SSM1-08	Autumn Wonders Gr. 1
SSN1-41	Baby Sister for Frances NS 1-3
SSPC-19	Back to School B/W Pictures
SSC1-33	Back to School Gr. 2-3
SSN1-224	Banner in the Sky NS 7-8
SSN1-36	Bargain for Frances NS 1-3
SSB1-82	Bats Gr. 4-6
SSN1-71	BB – Drug Free Zone NS Gr. 1-3
SSN1-88	BB – In the Freaky House NS 1-3
SSN1-78	BB – Media Madness NS 1-3
SSN1-69	BB – Wheelchair Commando NS 1-3
SSN1-119	Be a Perfect Person-3 Days NS 4-6
SSC1-15	Be My Valentine Gr. 1
SSD1-01	Be Safe Not Sorry Gr. P-1
SSN1-09	Bear Tales Gr. 2-4
SSB1-28	Bears Gr. 4-6
SSN1-202	Bears in Literature Gr. 1-3
SSN1-40	Beatrix Potter Gr. 2-4
SSN1-129	Beatrix Potter: Activity Biography 2-4
SSB1-47	Beautiful Bugs Gr. 1
SSB1-21	Beavers Gr. 3-5
SSN1-257	Because of Winn-Dixie NS Gr. 4-6
SSN1-33	Bedtime for Frances NS 1-3
SSN1-114	Best Christmas Pageant Ever NS 4-6
SSN1-32	Best Friends for Frances NS 1-3
SSB1-39	Best Friends Pets Gr. P-K
SSN1-185	BFG NS Gr. 4-6
SSN1-35	Birthday for Frances NS Gr. 1-3
SSN1-107	Borrowers NS Gr. 4-6
SSC1-16	Bouquet of Valentines Gr. 2
SSN1-29	Bread & Jam for Frances NS 1-3
SSN1-63	Bridge to Terabithia NS Gr. 4-6
SSY1-24	BTS Numeración Gr. 1-3
SSY1-25	BTS Adición Gr. 1-3
SSY1-26	BTS Sustracción Gr. 1-3
SSY1-27	BTS Fonética Gr. 1-3
SSY1-28	BTS Leer para Entender Gr. 1-3
SSY1-29	BTS Uso de las Mayúsculas y Reglas de Puntuación Gr. 1-3
SSY1-30	BTS Composición de Oraciones Gr. 1-3
SSY1-31	BTS Composici13n de Historias Gr. 1-3
SSN1-256	Bud, Not Buddy NS Gr. 4-6
SSB1-31	Bugs, Bugs & More Bugs Gr. 2-3
SSR1-07	Building Word Families L.V. 1-2
SSR1-05	Building Word Families S.V. 1-2
SSN1-204	Bunnicula NS Gr. 4-6
SSB1-80	Butterflies & Caterpillars Gr. 1-2
SSN1-164	Call It Courage NS Gr. 7-8
SSN1-67	Call of the Wild NS Gr. 7-8
SSJ1-41	Canada & It's Trading Partners 6-8
SSPC-28	Canada B/W Pictures
SSN1-173	Canada Geese Quilt NS Gr. 4-6
SSJ1-01	Canada Gr. 1
SSJ1-33	Canada's Capital Cities Gr. 4-6
SSJ1-43	Canada's Confederation Gr. 7-8
SSF1-04	Canada's First Nations Gr. 7-8
SSJ1-51	Canada's Landmarks Gr. 1-3
SSJ1-48	Canada's Landmarks Gr. 4-6
SSJ1-42	Canada's Traditions & Celeb. Gr. 1-3
SSB1-45	Canadian Animals Gr. 1-2
SSJ1-37	Canadian Arctic Inuit Gr. 2-3
SSJ1-53	Canadian Black History Gr. 4-8
SSJ1-57	Canadian Comprehension Gr. 1-2
SSJ1-58	Canadian Comprehension Gr. 3-4
SSJ1-59	Canadian Comprehension Gr. 5-6
SSJ1-46	Canadian Industries Gr. 4-6
SSK1-12	Canadian Problem Solving Gr. 4-6
SSJ1-38	Canadian Provinces & Terr. Gr. 4-6
SSY1-07	Capitalization & Punctuation Gr. 1-3
SSN1-198	Captain Courageous NS Gr. 7-8
SSK1-11	Cars Problem Solving Gr. 3-4
SSN1-154	Castle in the Attic NS Gr. 4-6
SSF1-31	Castles & Kings Gr. 4-6
SSN1-144	Cat Ate My Gymsuit NS Gr. 4-6
SSPC-38	Cats B/W Pictures
SSB1-50	Cats – Domestic & Wild Gr. 4-6
SSN1-34	Cats in Literature Gr. 3-6
SSN1-212	Cay NS Gr. 7-8
SSM1-09	Celebrate Autumn Gr. 4-6
SSC1-39	Celebrate Christmas Gr. 4-6
SSC1-31	Celebrate Easter Gr. 4-6
SSC1-23	Celebrate Shamrock Day Gr. 2
SSM1-11	Celebrate Spring Gr. 4-6
SSC1-13	Celebrate Thanksgiving R. 3-4
SSM1-06	Celebrate Winter Gr. 4-6
SSB1-107	Cells, Tissues & Organs Gr. 7-8
SSB1-101	Characteristics of Flight Gr. 4-6
SSN1-66	Charlie & Chocolate Factory NS 4-6
SSN1-23	Charlotte's Web NS Gr. 4-6
SSB1-37	Chicks N'Ducks Gr. 2-4
SSA1-09	China Today Gr. 5-8
SSN1-70	Chocolate Fever NS Gr. 4-6
SSN1-241	Chocolate Touch NS Gr. 4-6
SSC1-38	Christmas Around the World Gr. 4-6
SSPC-42	Christmas B/W Pictures
SST1-08A	Christmas Gr. JK/SK
SST1-08B	Christmas Gr. 1
SST1-08C	Christmas Gr. 2-3
SSC1-04	Christmas Magic Gr. 1
SSC1-03	Christmas Tales Gr. 2-3
SSG1-06	Cinematography Gr. 5-8
SSPC-13	Circus B/W Pictures
SSF1-03	Circus Magic Gr. 3-4
SSJ1-52	Citizenship/Immigration Gr. 4-8
SSN1-104	Classical Poetry Gr. 7-12
SSN1-227	Color Gr. 1-3
SSN1-203	Colour Gr. 1-3
SSN1-135	Come Back Amelia Bedelia NS 1-3
SSH1-11	Community Helpers Gr. 1-3
SSK1-02	Concept Cards & Activities Gr. P-1
SSN1-183	Copper Sunrise NS Gr. 7-8
SSN1-86	Corduroy & Pocket Corduroy NS 1-3
SSN1-124	Could Dracula Live in Wood NS 4-6
SSN1-148	Cowboy's Don't Cry NS Gr. 7-8
SSR1-01	Creativity with Food Gr. 4-8
SSB1-34	Creatures of the Sea Gr. 2-4
SSN1-208	Curse of the Viking Grave NS 7-8
SSN1-134	Danny Champion of World NS 4-6
SSN1-98	Danny's Run NS Gr. 7-8
SSK1-21	Data Management Gr. 4-6
SSB1-53	Dealing with Dinosaurs Gr. 4-6
SSN1-178	Dear Mr. Henshaw NS Gr. 4-6
SSB1-22	Deer Gr. 3-5
SSPC-20	Desert B/W Pictures
SSJ1-40	Development of Western Canada Gr. 7-8
SSA1-16	Development of Manufacturing 7-9
SSN1-105	Dicken's Christmas NS Gr. 7-8
SSN1-62	Different Dragons NS Gr. 4-6
SSPC-21	Dinosaurs B/W Pictures
SSB1-16	Dinosaurs Gr. 1
SST1-02A	Dinosaurs Gr. JK/SK
SST1-02B	Dinosaurs Gr. 1
SST1-02C	Dinosaurs Gr. 2-3
SSN1-175	Dinosaurs in Literature Gr. 1-3
SSJ1-26	Discover Nova Scotia Gr. 5-7
SSJ1-36	Discover Nunavut Territory Gr. 5-7
SSJ1-25	Discover Ontario Gr. 5-7
SSJ1-24	Discover PEI Gr. 5-7
SSJ1-22	Discover Québec Gr. 5-7
SSL1-01	Discovering the Library Gr. 2-3
SSB1-106	Diversity of Living Things Gr. 4-6
SSK1-27	Division Drills Gr. 4-6
SSB1-30	Dogs – Wild & Tame Gr. 4-6
SSPC-31	Dogs B/W Pictures
SSN1-196	Dog's Don't Tell Jokes NS Gr. 4-6
SSN1-182	Door in the Wall NS Gr. 4-6
SSB1-87	Down by the Sea Gr. 1-3
SSN1-189	Dr. Jeckyll & Mr. Hyde NS Gr. 4-6
SSG1-07	Dragon Trivia Gr. P-8
SSN1-102	Dragon's Egg NS Gr. 4-6
SSN1-16	Dragons in Literature Gr. 3-6
SSC1-06	Early Christmas Gr. 3-5
SSB1-109	Earth's Crust Gr. 6-8
SSC1-21	Easter Adventures Gr. 3-4
SSC1-17	Easter Delights Gr. P-K
SSC1-19	Easter Surprises Gr. 1
SSPC-12	Egypt B/W Pictures
SSN1-255	Egypt Game NS Gr. 4-6
SSF1-28	Egyptians Today & Yesterday Gr. 2-3
SSJ1-49	Elections in Canada Gr. 4-8
SSB1-108	Electricity Gr. 4-6
SSN1-02	Elves & the Shoemaker NS Gr. 1-3
SSH1-14	Emotions Gr. P-2
SSB1-85	Energy Gr. 4-6
SSN1-108	English Language Gr. 10-12
SSN1-156	Enjoying Eric Wilson Series Gr. 5-7
SSB1-64	Environment Gr. 4-6
SSR1-12	ESL Teaching Ideas Gr. K-8
SSN1-258	Esperanza Rising NS Gr. 4-6
SSR1-22	Exercises in Grammar Gr. 6
SSR1-23	Exercises in Grammar Gr. 7
SSR1-24	Exercises in Grammar Gr. 8
SSF1-20	Exploration Gr. 4-6
SSF1-15	Explorers & Mapmakers of Canada 7-8
SSJ1-54	Exploring Canada Gr. 1-3
SSJ1-56	Exploring Canada Gr. 1-6
SSJ1-55	Exploring Canada Gr. 4-6
SSH1-20	Exploring My School and Community Gr. 1
SSPC-39	Fables B/W Pictures
SSN1-15	Fables Gr. 4-6
SSN1-04	Fairy Tale Magic Gr. 3-5
SSPC-11	Fairy Tales B/W Pictures
SSN1-11	Fairy Tales Gr. 1-2
SSN1-199	Family Under the Bridge NS 4-6
SSPC-41	Famous Canadians B/W Pictures
SSJ1-12	Famous Canadians Gr. 4-8
SSN1-210	Fantastic Mr. Fox NS Gr. 4-6
SSB1-36	Fantastic Plants Gr. 4-6
SSPC-04	Farm Animals B/W Pictures
SSB1-15	Farm Animals Gr. 1-2
SST1-03A	Farm Gr. JK/SK
SST1-03B	Farm Gr. 1
SST1-03C	Farm Gr. 2-3
SSJ1-05	Farming Community Gr. 3-4
SSB1-44	Farmyard Friends Gr. P-K
SSJ1-45	Fathers of Confederation Gr. 4-8
SSB1-19	Feathered Friends Gr. 4-6
SST1-05A	February Gr. JK/SK
SST1-05B	February Gr. 1
SST1-05C	February Gr. 2-3
SSN1-03	Festival of Fairytales Gr. 3-5
SSC1-36	Festivals Around the World Gr. 2-3
SSN1-168	First 100 Sight Words Gr. 1
SSC1-32	First Days at School Gr. 1
SSJ1-06	Fishing Community Gr. 3-4
SSN1-170	Flowers for Algernon NS Gr. 7-8
SSN1-128	Fly Away Home NS Gr. 4-6
SSD1-05	Food: Fact, Fun & Fiction Gr. 1-3
SSD1-06	Food: Nutrition & Invention Gr. 4-6
SSB1-118	Force and Motion Gr. 1-3
SSB1-119	Force and Motion Gr. 4-6
SSB1-25	Foxes Gr. 3-5
SSN1-172	Freckle Juice NS Gr. 1-3
SSB1-43	Friendly Frogs Gr. 1
SSB1-89	Fruits & Seeds Gr. 4-6
SSN1-137	Fudge-a-Mania NS Gr. 4-6
SSB1-14	Fun on the Farm Gr. 3-4
SSR1-49	Fun with Phonics Gr. 1-3
SSPC-06	Garden Flowers B/W Pictures
SSK1-03	Geometric Shapes Gr. 2-5
SSC1-18	Get the Rabbit Habit Gr. 1-2
SSN1-209	Giver, The NS Gr. 7-8
SSN1-190	Go Jump in the Pool NS Gr. 4-6
SSG1-03	Goal Setting Gr. 6-8
SSG1-08	Gr. 3 Test – Parent Guide
SSG1-99	Gr. 3 Test – Teacher Guide
SSG1-09	Gr. 6 Language Test – Parent Guide
SSG1-97	Gr. 6 Language Test – Teacher Guide
SSG1-10	Gr. 6 Math Test – Parent Guide
SSG1-96	Gr. 6 Math Test – Teacher Guide
SSG1-98	Gr. 6 Math/Lang. Test – Teacher Guide
SSK1-14	Graph for all Seasons Gr. 1-3
SSN1-117	Great Brain NS Gr. 4-6
SSN1-90	Great Expectations NS Gr. 7-8
SSN1-169	Great Gilly Hopkins NS Gr. 4-6
SSN1-197	Great Science Fair Disaster NS 4-6
SSN1-138	Greek Mythology Gr. 7-8
SSN1-113	Green Gables Detectives NS 4-6
SSC1-26	Groundhog Celebration Gr. 2
SSC1-25	Groundhog Day Gr. 1
SSB1-113	Growth & Change in Animals Gr. 2-3
SSB1-114	Growth & Change in Plants Gr. 2-3
SSB1-48	Guinea Pigs & Friends Gr. 3-5
SSB1-104	Habitats Gr. 4-6
SSPC-18	Halloween B/W Pictures
SST1-04A	Halloween Gr. JK/SK
SST1-04B	Halloween Gr. 1
SST1-04C	Halloween Gr. 2-3
SSC1-10	Halloween Gr. 4-6
SSC1-08	Halloween Happiness Gr. 1
SSC1-29	Halloween Spirits Gr. P-K
SSC1-42	Happy Valentines Day Gr. 3
SSN1-205	Harper Moon NS Gr. 7-8
SSN1-123	Harriet the Spy NS Gr. 4-6
SSC1-11	Harvest Time Wonders Gr. 1
SSN1-136	Hatchet NS Gr. 7-8
SSC1-09	Haunting Halloween Gr. 2-3
SSN1-91	Hawk & Stretch NS Gr. 4-6
SSC1-30	Hearts & Flowers Gr. P-K
SSN1-22	Heidi NS Gr. 4-6
SSN1-120	Help I'm Trapped in My NS 4-6
SSN1-24	Henry & the Clubhouse NS 4-6
SSN1-184	Hobbit NS Gr. 7-8
SSN1-122	Hoboken Chicken Emerg. NS 4-6
SSN1-250	Holes NS Gr. 4-6
SSN1-116	How Can a Frozen Detective NS 4-6
SSN1-89	How Can I be a Detective if I NS 4-6
SSN1-96	How Come the Best Clues... NS 4-6
SSN1-133	How To Eat Fried Worms NS 4-6
SSR1-48	How To Give a Presentation Gr. 4-6
SSN1-125	How To Teach Writing Through 7-9
SSR1-10	How To Write a Composition 6-10
SSR1-09	How To Write a Paragraph 5-10
SSR1-08	How To Write an Essay Gr. 7-12
SSR1-03	How To Write Poetry & Stories 4-6
SSD1-07	Human Body Gr. 2-4
SSD1-02	Human Body Gr. 4-6
SSN1-25	I Want to Go Home NS Gr. 4-6
SSH1-06	I'm Important Gr. 2-3
SSH1-07	I'm Unique Gr. 4-6

Publication Listing

Code #	Title and Grade
SSF1-05	In Days of Yore Gr. 4-6
SSF1-06	In Pioneer Days Gr. 2-4
SSM1-10	In the Wintertime Gr. 2
SSB1-41	Incredible Dinosaurs Gr. P-1
SSN1-177	Incredible Journey NS Gr. 4-6
SSN1-100	Indian in the Cupboard NS Gr. 4-6
SSPC-05	Insects B/W Pictures
SSPC-10	Inuit B/W Pictures
SSJ1-10	Inuit Community Gr. 3-4
SSN1-85	Ira Sleeps Over NS Gr. 1-3
SSN1-93	Iron Man NS Gr. 4-6
SSN1-193	Island of the Blue Dolphins NS 4-6
SSB1-11	It's a Dogs World Gr. 2-3
SSM1-05	It's a Marshmallow World Gr. 3
SSK1-05	It's About Time Gr. 2-4
SSC1-41	It's Christmas Time Gr. 3
SSH1-04	It's Circus Time Gr. 1
SSC1-43	It's Groundhog Day Gr. 3
SSB1-75	It's Maple Syrup Time Gr. 2-4
SSC1-40	It's Trick or Treat Time Gr. 2
SSN1-65	James & The Giant Peach NS 4-6
SSN1-106	Jane Eyre NS Gr. 7-8
SSPC-25	Japan B/W Pictures
SSA1-06	Japan Gr. 5-8
SSC1-05	Joy of Christmas Gr. 2
SSN1-161	Julie of the Wolves NS Gr. 7-8
SSB1-81	Jungles Gr. 2-3
SSE1-02	Junior Music for Fall Gr. 4-6
SSE1-05	Junior Music for Spring Gr. 4-6
SSE1-06	Junior Music for Winter Gr. 4-6
SSN1-151	Kate NS Gr. 4-6
SSN1-95	Kidnapped in the Yukon NS Gr. 4-6
SSN1-140	Kids at Bailey School Gr. 2-4
SSN1-176	King of the Wind NS Gr. 4-6
SSF1-29	Klondike Gold Rush Gr. 4-6
SSF1-33	Labour Movement in Canada Gr. 7-8
SSN1-152	Lamplighter NS Gr. 4-6
SSB1-98	Learning About Dinosaurs Gr. 3
SSN1-38	Learning About Giants Gr. 4-6
SSK1-22	Learning About Measurement Gr. 1-3
SSB1-46	Learning About Mice Gr. 3-5
SSK1-09	Learning About Money CDN Gr. 1-3
SSK1-19	Learning About Money USA Gr. 1-3
SSK1-23	Learning About Numbers Gr. 1-3
SSB1-69	Learning About Rocks and Soils Gr. 2-3
SSK1-08	Learning About Shapes Gr. 1-3
SSB1-100	Learning About Simple Machines 1-3
SSK1-04	Learning About the Calendar Gr. 2-3
SSK1-10	Learning About Time Gr. 1-3
SSH1-17	Learning About Transportation Gr. 1
SSB1-02	Leaves Gr. 2-3
SSN1-50	Legends Gr. 4-6
SSC1-27	Lest We Forget Gr. 4-6
SSJ1-13	Let's Look at Canada Gr. 4-6
SSJ1-16	Let's Visit Alberta Gr. 2-4
SSJ1-15	Let's Visit British Columbia Gr. 2-4
SSJ1-03	Let's Visit Canada Gr. 3
SSJ1-18	Let's Visit Manitoba Gr. 2-4
SSJ1-21	Let's Visit New Brunswick Gr. 2-4
SSJ1-27	Let's Visit Newfoundland & Labrador Gr. 2-4
SSJ1-30	Let's Visit North West Terr. Gr. 2-4
SSJ1-20	Let's Visit Nova Scotia Gr. 2-4
SSJ1-34	Let's Visit Nunavut Gr. 2-4
SSJ1-17	Let's Visit Ontario Gr. 2-4
SSQ1-08	Let's Visit Ottawa Big Book Pkg 1-3
SSJ1-19	Let's Visit PEI Gr. 2-4
SSJ1-31	Let's Visit Québec Gr. 2-4
SSJ1-14	Let's Visit Saskatchewan Gr. 2-4
SSJ1-28	Let's Visit Yukon Gr. 2-4
SSN1-130	Life & Adv. of Santa Claus NS 7-8
SSB1-10	Life in a Pond Gr. 3-4
SSF1-30	Life in the Middle Ages Gr. 7-8
SSB1-103	Light & Sound Gr. 4-6
SSN1-219	Light in the Forest NS Gr. 7-8
SSN1-121	Light on Hogback Hill NS Gr. 4-6
SSN1-46	Lion, Witch & the Wardrobe NS 4-6
SSR1-51	Literature Response Forms Gr. 1-3
SSR1-52	Literature Response Forms Gr. 4-6
SSN1-28	Little House Big Woods NS 4-6
SSN1-233	Little House on the Prairie NS 4-6
SSN1-111	Little Women NS Gr. 7-8
SSN1-115	Live from the Fifth Grade NS 4-6
SSN1-141	Look Through My Window NS 4-6
SSN1-112	Look! Visual Discrimination Gr. P-1
SSN1-61	Lost & Found NS Gr. 4-6
SSN1-109	Lost in the Barrens NS Gr. 7-8
SSJ1-08	Lumbering Community Gr. 3-4
SSN1-167	Magic School Bus Gr. 1-3
SSN1-247	Magic Treehouse Gr. 1-3
SSB1-78	Magnets Gr. 3-5
SSD1-03	Making Sense of Our Senses K-1
SSN1-146	Mama's Going to Buy You a Mocking Bird NS 4-6
SSB1-94	Mammals Gr. 1
SSB1-95	Mammals Gr. 2
SSB1-96	Mammals Gr. 3
SSB1-97	Mammals Gr. 5-6
SSN1-160	Maniac Magee NS Gr. 4-6
SSA1-19	Mapping Activities & Outlines! 4-8
SSA1-17	Mapping Skills Gr. 1-3
SSA1-07	Mapping Skills Gr. 4-6
SST1-10A	March Gr. JK/SK
SST1-10B	March Gr. 1
SST1-10C	March Gr. 2-3
SSB1-57	Marvellous Marsupials Gr. 4-6
SSK1-01	Math Signs & Symbols Gr. 1-3
SSB1-116	Matter & Materials Gr. 1-3
SSB1-117	Matter & Materials Gr. 4-6
SSH1-03	Me, I'm Special! Gr. P-1
SSK1-16	Measurement Gr. 4-8
SSC1-02	Medieval Christmas Gr. 4-6
SSPC-09	Medieval Life B/W Pictures
SSC1-07	Merry Christmas Gr. P-K
SSK1-15	Metric Measurement Gr. 4-8
SSN1-13	Mice in Literature Gr. 3-5
SSB1-70	Microscopy Gr. 4-6
SSN1-180	Midnight Fox NS Gr. 4-6
SSN1-243	Midwife's Apprentice NS Gr. 4-6
SSJ1-07	Mining Community Gr. 3-4
SSK1-17	Money Talks – Cdn Gr. 3-6
SSK1-18	Money Talks – USA Gr. 3-6
SSB1-56	Monkeys & Apes Gr. 4-6
SSN1-43	Monkeys in Literature Gr. 2-4
SSN1-54	Monster Mania Gr. 4-6
SSN1-97	Mouse & the Motorcycle NS 4-6
SSN1-94	Mr. Poppers Penguins NS Gr. 4-6
SSN1-201	Mrs. Frisby & Rats NS Gr. 4-6
SSR1-13	Milti-Level Spelling Program Gr. 3-6
SSR1-26	Multi-Level Spelling USA Gr. 3-6
SSK1-31	Addition & Subtraction Drills 1-3
SSK1-32	Multiplication & Division Drills 4-6
SSK1-30	Multiplication Drills Gr. 4-6
SSA1-14	My Country! The USA! Gr. 2-4
SSN1-186	My Side of the Mountain NS 7-8
SSN1-58	Mysteries, Monsters & Magic Gr. 6-8
SSN1-37	Mystery at Blackrock Island NS 7-8
SSN1-80	Mystery House NS 4-6
SSN1-157	Nate the Great & Sticky Case NS 1-3
SSF1-23	Native People of North America 4-6
SSF1-25	New France Part 1 Gr. 7-8
SSF1-27	New France Part 2 Gr. 7-8
SSA1-10	New Zealand Gr. 4-8
SSN1-51	Newspapers Gr. 5-8
SSN1-47	No Word for Goodbye NS Gr. 7-8
SSPC-03	North American Animals B/W Pictures
SSF1-22	North American Natives Gr. 2-4
SSN1-75	Novel Ideas Gr. 4-6
SST1-06A	November JK/SK
SST1-06B	November Gr. 1
SST1-06C	November Gr. 2-3
SSN1-244	Number the Stars NS Gr. 4-6
SSY1-03	Numeration Gr. 1-3
SSPC-14	Nursery Rhymes B/W Pictures
SSN1-12	Nursery Rhymes Gr. P-1
SSN1-59	On the Banks of Plum Creek NS 4-6
SSN1-220	One in Middle Green Kangaroo NS 1-3
SSN1-145	One to Grow On NS Gr. 4-6
SSB1-27	Opossums Gr. 3-5
SSJ1-23	Ottawa Gr. 7-9
SSJ1-39	Our Canadian Governments Gr. 5-8
SSF1-14	Our Global Heritage Gr. 4-6
SSH1-12	Our Neighbourhoods Gr. 4-6
SSB1-72	Our Trash Gr. 2-3
SSB1-51	Our Universe Gr. 5-8
SSB1-86	Outer Space Gr. 1-2
SSA1-18	Outline Maps of the World Gr. 1-8
SSB1-67	Owls Gr. 4-6
SSN1-31	Owls in the Family NS Gr. 4-6
SSL1-02	Oxbridge Owl & The Library Gr. 4-6
SSB1-71	Pandas, Polar & Penguins Gr. 4-6
SSN1-52	Paperbag Princess NS Gr. 1-3
SSR1-11	Passion of Jesus: A Play Gr. 7-8
SSA1-12	Passport to Adventure Gr. 4-5
SSR1-06	Passport to Adventure Gr. 7-8
SSR1-04	Personal Spelling Dictionary Gr. 2-5
SSPC-29	Pets B/W Pictures
SSE1-03	Phantom of the Opera Gr. 7-9
SSN1-171	Phoebe Gilman Author Study Gr. 2-3
SSY1-06	Phonics Gr. 1-3
SSN1-237	Pierre Berton Author Study Gr. 7-8
SSN1-179	Pigman NS Gr. 7-8
SSN1-48	Pigs in Literature Gr. 2-4
SSN1-99	Pinballs NS Gr. 4-6
SSN1-60	Pippi Longstocking NS Gr. 4-6
SSF1-12	Pirates Gr. 4-6
SSK1-13	Place Value Gr. 4-6
SSB1-77	Planets Gr. 3-6
SSB1-66	Popcorn Fun Gr. 2-3
SSB1-20	Porcupines Gr. 3-5
SSF1-24	Prehistoric Times Gr. 4-6
SSE1-01	Primary Music for Fall Gr. 1-3
SSE1-04	Primary Music for Spring Gr. 1-3
SSE1-07	Primary Music for Winter Gr. 1-3
SSJ1-47	Prime Ministers of Canada Gr. 4-8
SSK1-20	Probability & Inheritance Gr. 7-10
SSN1-49	Question of Loyalty NS Gr. 7-8
SSN1-26	Rabbits in Literature Gr. 2-4
SSB1-17	Raccoons Gr. 3-5
SSN1-207	Radio Fifth Grade NS Gr. 4-6
SSB1-52	Rainbow of Colours Gr. 4-6
SSN1-144	Ramona Quimby Age 8 NS 4-6
SSJ1-09	Ranching Community Gr. 3-4
SSY1-08	Reading for Meaning Gr. 1-3
SSN1-165	Reading Response Forms Gr. 1-3
SSN1-239	Reading Response Forms Gr. 4-6
SSN1-234	Reading with Arthur Gr. 1-3
SSN1-249	Reading with Canadian Authors 1-3
SSN1-200	Reading with Curious George 2-4
SSN1-230	Reading with Eric Carle Gr. 1-3
SSN1-251	Reading with Kenneth Oppel 4-6
SSN1-127	Reading with Mercer Mayer 1-2
SSN1-07	Reading with Motley Crew Gr. 2-3
SSN1-142	Reading with Robert Munsch 1-3
SSN1-06	Reading with the Super Sleuths 4-6
SSN1-08	Reading with the Ziggles Gr. 1
SST1-11A	Red Gr. JK/SK
SSN1-147	Refuge NS Gr. 7-8
SSC1-44	Remembrance Day Gr. 1-3
SSPC-23	Reptiles B/W Pictures
SSB1-42	Reptiles Gr. 4-6
SSN1-110	Return of the Indian NS Gr. 4-6
SSN1-225	River NS Gr. 7-8
SSE1-08	Robert Schuman, Composer Gr. 6-9
SSN1-83	Robot Alert NS Gr. 4-6
SSB1-65	Rocks & Minerals Gr. 4-6
SSN1-149	Romeo & Juliet NS Gr. 7-8
SSB1-88	Romping Reindeer Gr. K-3
SSN1-21	Rumplestiltskin NS Gr. 1-3
SSN1-153	Runaway Ralph NS Gr. 4-6
SSN1-103	Sadako and 1 000 Paper Cranes NS 4-6
SSD1-04	Safety Gr. 2-4
SSN1-42	Sarah Plain & Tall NS Gr. 4-6
SSC1-34	School in September Gr. 4-6
SSPC-01	Sea Creatures B/W Pictures
SSB1-79	Sea Creatures Gr. 1-3
SSN1-64	Secret Garden NS Gr. 4-6
SSB1-90	Seeds & Weeds Gr. 2-3
SSY1-02	Sentence Writing Gr. 1-3
SST1-07A	September JK/SK
SST1-07B	September Gr. 1
SST1-07C	September Gr. 2-3
SSN1-30	Serendipity Series Gr. 3-5
SSC1-22	Shamrocks on Parade Gr. 1
SSC1-24	Shamrocks, Harps & Shillelaghs 3-4
SSR1-66	Shakespeare Shorts – Performing Arts Gr. 2-4
SSR1-67	Shakespeare Shorts – Performing Arts Gr. 4-6
SSR1-68	Shakespeare Shorts – Language Arts Gr. 2-4
SSR1-69	Shakespeare Shorts – Language Arts Gr. 4-6
SSB1-74	Sharks Gr. 4-6
SSN1-158	Shiloh NS Gr. 4-6
SSN1-84	Sideways Stories Wayside NS 4-6
SSN1-181	Sight Words Activities Gr. 1
SSB1-99	Simple Machines Gr. 4-6
SSN1-19	Sixth Grade Secrets 4-6
SSG1-04	Skill Building with Slates Gr. K-8
SSN1-118	Skinny Bones NS Gr. 4-6
SSB1-24	Skunks Gr. 3-5
SSN1-191	Sky is Falling NS Gr. 4-6
SSB1-83	Slugs & Snails Gr. 1-3
SSB1-55	Snakes Gr. 4-6
SST1-12A	Snow Gr. JK/SK
SST1-12B	Snow Gr. 1
SST1-12C	Snow Gr. 2-3
SSB1-76	Solar System Gr. 4-6
SSPC-44	South America B/W Pictures
SSA1-11	South America Gr. 4-6
SSB1-05	Space Gr. 2-3
SSR1-34	Spelling Blacklines Gr. 1
SSR1-35	Spelling Blacklines Gr. 2
SSR1-14	Spelling Gr. 1
SSR1-15	Spelling Gr. 2
SSR1-16	Spelling Gr. 3
SSR1-17	Spelling Gr. 4
SSR1-18	Spelling Gr. 5
SSR1-19	Spelling Gr. 6
SSR1-27	Spelling Worksavers #1 Gr. 3-5
SSM1-02	Spring Celebration Gr. 2-3
SST1-01A	Spring Gr. JK/SK
SST1-01B	Spring Gr. 1
SST1-01C	Spring Gr. 2-3
SSM1-01	Spring in the Garden Gr. 1-2
SSB1-26	Squirrels Gr. 3-5
SSB1-112	Stable Structures and Mechanisms Gr. 3
SSG1-05	Steps in the Research Process 5-8
SSG1-02	Stock Market Gr. 7-8
SSN1-139	Stone Fox NS Gr. 4-6
SSN1-214	Stone Orchard NS Gr. 7-8
SSN1-01	Story Book Land of Witches Gr. 2-3
SSR1-64	Story Starters Gr. 1-3
SSR1-65	Story Starters Gr. 4-6
SSR1-73	Story Starters Gr. 1-6
SSY1-09	Story Writing Gr. 1-3
SSB1-111	Structures, Mechanisms and Motion Gr. 2
SSN1-211	Stuart Little NS Gr. 4-6
SSK1-29	Subtraction Drills Gr. 1-3
SSY1-05	Subtraction Gr. 1-3
SSY1-11	Successful Language Pract. Gr. 1-3
SSY1-12	Successful Math Practice Gr. 1-3
SSW1-09	Summer Learning Gr. K-1
SSW1-10	Summer Learning Gr. 1-2
SSW1-11	Summer Learning Gr. 2-3
SSW1-12	Summer Learning Gr. 3-4
SSW1-13	Summer Learning Gr. 4-5
SSW1-14	Summer Learning Gr. 5-6
SSN1-159	Summer of the Swans NS Gr. 4-6
SSZ1-02	Summer Olympics Gr. 4-6
SSM1-07	Super Summer Gr. 1-2
SSN1-18	Superfudge NS Gr. 4-6
SSA1-08	Switzerland Gr. 4-6
SSN1-20	T.V. Kid NS. Gr. 4-6
SSA1-15	Take a Trip to Australia Gr. 2-3
SSB1-102	Taking Off With Flight Gr. 1-3
SSN1-55	Tales of the Fourth Grade NS 4-6
SSN1-188	Taste of Blackberries NS Gr. 4-6
SSK1-07	Teaching Math Through Sports 6-9
SST1-09A	Thanksgiving JK/SK
SST1-09C	Thanksgiving Gr. 2-3
SSN1-77	There's a Boy in the Girls... NS 4-6
SSN1-143	This Can't Be Happening NS 4-6
SSN1-05	Three Billy Goats Gruff NS Gr. 1-3
SSN1-72	Ticket to Curlew NS Gr. 4-6
SSN1-82	Timothy of the Cay NS Gr. 7-8
SSF1-32	Titanic Gr. 4-6
SSN1-222	To Kill a Mockingbird NS Gr. 7-8
SSN1-195	Toilet Paper Tigers NS Gr. 4-6
SSJ1-35	Toronto Gr. 4-8
SSH1-02	Toy Shelf Gr. P-K
SSPC-24	Toys B/W Pictures
SSN1-163	Traditional Poetry Gr. 7-10
SSH1-13	Transportation Gr. 4-6
SSW1-01	Transportation Snip Art
SSB1-03	Trees Gr. 2-3
SSA1-01	Tropical Rainforest Gr. 4-6
SSN1-56	Trumpet of the Swan NS Gr. 4-6
SSN1-81	Tuck Everlasting NS Gr. 4-6
SSN1-126	Turtles in Literature Gr. 1-3
SSN1-45	Underground to Canada NS 4-6
SSN1-27	Unicorns in Literature Gr. 3-5
SSJ1-44	Upper & Lower Canada Gr. 7-8
SSN1-192	Using Novels Canadian North Gr. 7-8
SSC1-14	Valentines Day Gr. 5-8
SSPC-45	Vegetables B/W Pictures
SSY1-01	Very Hungry Caterpillar NS 30/Pkg 1-3
SSF1-13	Victorian Era Gr. 7-8
SSC1-35	Victorian Christmas Gr. 5-8
SSF1-17	Viking Age Gr. 4-6
SSN1-206	War with Grandpa SN Gr. 4-6
SSB1-91	Water Gr. 2-4
SSN1-166	Watership Down NS Gr. 7-8
SSH1-16	Ways We Travel Gr. P-K
SSN1-101	Wayside School Gets a Little Stranger NS 4-6

Code #	Title and Grade	Code #	Title and Grade	Code #	Title and Grade	Code #	Title and Grade
SSN1-76	Wayside School is Falling Down NS 4-6						
SSB1-60	Weather Gr. 4-6						
SSN1-17	Wee Folk in Literature Gr. 3-5						
SSPC-08	Weeds B/W Pictures						
SSQ1-04	Welcome Back – Big Book Pkg 1-3						
SSB1-73	Whale Preservation Gr. 5-8						
SSH1-08	What is a Community? Gr. 2-4						
SSH1-01	What is a Family? Gr. 2-3						
SSH1-09	What is a School? Gr. 1-2						
SSJ1-32	What is Canada? Gr. P-K						
SSN1-79	What is RAD? Read and Discover 2-4						
SSB1-62	What is the Weather Today? Gr. 2-4						
SSN1-194	What's a Daring Detective NS 4-6						
SSH1-10	What's My Number Gr. P-K						
SSR1-02	What's the Scoop on Words Gr. 4-6						
SSN1-73	Where the Red Fern Grows NS 7-8						
SSN1-87	Where the Wild Things Are NS 1-3						
SSN1-187	Whipping Boy NS Gr. 4-6						
SSN1-226	Who is Frances Rain? NS Gr. 4-6						
SSN1-74	Who's Got Gertie & How...? NS 4-6						
SSN1-131	Why did the Underwear ... NS 4-6						
SSC1-28	Why Wear a Poppy? Gr. 2-3						
SSJ1-11	Wild Animals of Canada Gr. 2-3						
SSPC-07	Wild Flowers B/W Pictures						
SSB1-18	Winter Birds Gr. 2-3						
SSZ1-03	Winter Olympics Gr. 4-6						
SSM1-04	Winter Wonderland Gr. 1						
SSC1-01	Witches Gr. 3-4						
SSN1-213	Wolf Island NS Gr. 1-3						
SSE1-09	Wolfgang Amadeus Mozart 6-9						
SSB1-23	Wolves Gr. 3-5						
SSC1-20	Wonders of Easter Gr. 2						
SSB1-35	World of Horses Gr. 4-6						
SSB1-13	World of Pets Gr. 2-3						
SSF1-26	World War II Gr. 7-8						
SSN1-221	Wrinkle in Time NS Gr. 7-8						
SSPC-02	Zoo Animals B/W Pictures						
SSB1-08	Zoo Animals Gr. 1-2						
SSB1-09	Zoo Celebration Gr. 3-4						